Ethics For Executives

ETHICS FOR EXECUTIVES

Samuel Southard

Thomas Nelson, Inc., Publishers
New York/Camden/Nashville

Copyright © 1975 by Samuel Southard

All rights reserved under International and
Pan-American Conventions. Published in
Nashville, Tennessee, by Thomas Nelson, Inc., Publishers.

Manufactured in the United States of America.

Library of Congress Cataloging in Publication Data
Southard, Samuel.
    Ethics for executives.
    Bibliography: p.
    1. Executives—Conduct of life. I. Title.
HF5500.2.S694   174   74-26946
ISBN 0-8407-5588-0 (pbk.)
        0-8407-4042-5

To George Stoll, Sr.
and
Richard Wood,

Executives in the business and professional world who not only gave their time and money to help others, but were my inspiring and wise teachers of social concern and community planning through the Louisville and the Kentucky Council of Churches committees on public institutions.

Contents

Preface

We Americans are a great and diverse people. We take full advantage of our right to develop wide-ranging interests and responsibilities. For instance, I am a farmer, an engineer, a businessman, a planner, a scientist, a governor, and a Christian.

I don't believe there is any inherent conflict between these roles. There is no need to have a different set of standards as we develop commitments to our family, our neighbors, our customers, our clients, our constituents, or to Christ.

The only potential conflict we all face is one that we create ourselves—one caused when we are not willing to relinquish worldly prestige, possessions, and social prominence in order to accept without reticence the strictest ethical restraints.

There is a great tendency for all of us to shy away from difficult decisions and controversial issues. But every issue that is important and significant is bound to be controversial. Too often we avoid taking a stand for what we know to be right because we fear we will lose a dollar, or a client, or a vote. And in that moment we profess our willingness to trade that friend or that client for a relatively worthless temporary advantage. A habit of this is permanently debilitating.

No city, no state, no country can benefit from men in the professions, business or in politics who are more concerned about controversy than their conscience.

As Americans in this tough, competitive world, we are trained to be aggressive, manly, and unafraid. Because of this, we have developed a pride in our own toughness, and thus our priorities have sometimes become distorted.

We are inclined to conceal emotion, to exalt ourselves, and even to dwell on the mistakes of others. We assume the pharisaic attitude of saying, "Here I am, Lord, a member of the community's most prestigious church. I am proud that my devout attitude has enhanced my status as a politician and a businessman. Thank you for my clean reputation." It is not our custom to say, "Lord, I am not worthy to lift my eyes to heaven. Have mercy on me, a sinner."

As a Sunday school teacher since I was 18 years old, I have always known that the structure of society and its laws are founded on the Christian ethic that you shall love the Lord your God and your neighbor as yourself—a very high and perfect standard. However, the fallibility of man and the contentions in society don't permit us to achieve perfection. We do strive sporadically for excellence, but not with a fervent and daily commitment.

We who form the leadership of a community should exemplify the highest attributes of mankind, and never the lowest common denominator. In every component of life we should continually strive for perfection as commanded by God.

As a public servant who affects the lives of almost five million Georgians, I find a tremendous opportunity and obligation to use to the fullest extent whatever talents God has given me. However, all of us have similar opportunities and obligations in the perspective of our personal lives—whether it be in business, government, community, or home.

If we are truly concerned about the integrity of our lives—if we are willing to make an effort to devote our talents and resources to those things which are larger than ourselves—then there is no limit to what we can accomplish in the building of a fruitful and enjoyable existence.

JIMMY CARTER
Governor, State of Georgia

December, 1974

Introduction

Can executives be ethical in the competitive world of business or the power plays of public administration?

The question may seem old-fashioned to the cynical among our generation. It may seem self-evident to the moralist. It may seem unnecessary to the ruthless. But to the thousands of sensitive and lonely men (and women!) who really run the modern world—whether they be at the top of the organizational charts or in middle management —the question is painfully personal. Ethics, after all, are at the very heart of personal integrity, and personal integrity has traditionally been considered vastly more crucial for the decision maker—which is what an executive is—than for the person who carries out decisions.

The moral character of the executive has a direct influence upon the psychological climate of the entire agency.

The more authority a manager possesses, the greater is the impact of his character in the organization. He must combine the prudent use of power with sensitivity to the motivation of persons. Morality in management is a problem in distribution. Who is to be rewarded by receiving more and who is to be punished by receiving less? When a decision is made, the moral fibre of the manager is seen in his steadfastness. He must be brave as well as just.

But, can an executive be ethical in today's world?

Can Executives Be Ethical?

When executive readers of *Harvard Business Review* were questioned about business ethics, four out of five affirmed the presence in their industry of practices which are generally accepted but are also unethical. An insurance executive mentioned preferential treatment through lavish entertainment. A consumer services manager had discovered kickbacks to purchasing department employees. A financial counselor detected payoffs to government officials. A mass communication executive confessed deliberate distortion of facts.*

The moral problems of an executive go straight to the heart of personal integrity. The controller of a large firm must decide how to handle "a good friend caught cheating on his expenses." A security salesman must decide whether or not to tell the whole truth when a customer approaches him with an idea that would be profitable to the salesman, but unwise for the customer.

Truth, loyalty, justice, steadfastness, and temperance are constantly required of those who make decisions about the lives of others. It seems that the higher a man's position

---

* Raymond C. Baumhart, "How Ethical Are Businessmen?", *Harvard Business Review,* July-August, 1961.

in the company hierarchy, the more value premises he must consider. As Manley Jones wrote in *Executive Decision Making,* a good executive is one who has the courage to base his decisions upon value premises as well as the facts that are supplied him by leaders from lower echelons.

But is it realistic to expect these "old-fashioned" virtues in the modern world of complexity and conformity? A young director, Herbert Porter, told Senator Howard Baker that he did not speak out against "dirty tricks" because of the fear of group pressure that would ensue. When the Senator asked why he had abrogated his own conscience, Mr. Porter's reply was: "Loyalty."

The Question of Inner Direction

Is the first loyalty of a manager to his company or to his conscience? David Riesman wrote in 1950 that the executives of business and finance are increasingly oriented toward the opinions of others. The "team player" pays close attention to the signals of others, which determine his own opinions. Only in the older professions of medicine or law does an executive still have a chance for inner direction. That is, he can live by the moral sense implanted early in his life by his elders and direct his work toward destined goals. But in business or finance, an executive listens more to the voices of others than he does to the conscience within.

Is Riesman right? The power of society over the individual is emphasized in management studies. Chris Argyris argues in *Personality and Organization* that the hierarchy of a business organization is unhealthy for mature people. Organizations produce states of dependency in employees at all levels. The view is similar to the classic phrase of Veblen, "trained incapacity," or to Dewey's "occupational psychosis." Any person who works in a large organization is going to be professionally deformed. He cannot make an independent decision based upon time-honored principles.

This pessimistic view is opposed by other management experts such as McFarland. McFarland admits that there are many constraints upon an individual in an organization, but there are other views of man which would say that individuals protect themselves against excessive conformity, resist real dependency, and continue to realize their own potential wherever possible. Support for this view increases as we hear the testimony of top level management. They are the persons who say that values are essential to success at the executive level. Perhaps this is true because they are more free to make decisions than others.

Although there are many examples of conformity and defective character among the technocrats of industry and government, most executives would probably agree with a conclusion of the classic study *The American Business Creed:* "The business creed makes the moral individual decisive." [1] American business continually emphasizes self-reliance, the importance of private business decisions, the dangers of collective dependence on the welfare state.

The Big Get By?

A cynic may say: "So what? All you have proved is that an executive does have some freedom to pursue his own goals. What he wants is more money and power at

---

[1] Francis Sutton, *The American Business Creed,* p. 252.

the expense of everyone else. He can get by with his immorality."

This view is certainly popular in a large school of writing. Consider Sinclair Lewis' early work *Babbitt,* or the later work of Cameron Hawley, *Executive Suite.* The higher the person climbs in the organization, the greater is assumed to be his lust for money and recognition. This view has often been reinforced by some of the older economic theories which have from the eighteenth century presented the businessman as a totally profit-seeking creature.

It is almost amusing to find through research studies that executives often agree with this view when they are talking about their competitors. In Baumhart's study, 70% believe that the "average executive" would hire one of his competitor's employees who knew the details of some important scientific discovery. But only 48% of the respondents said that they would make the same decisions for themselves.

When executives were questioned further about this double standard, they replied that an executive who acts unethically is doing so largely because of his superiors and the climate of industry ethics. The respondents must have believed that they were in a more ethical atmosphere than that of their competitors.

Managers are interested in something more than money. John Shallenberger, President of the Connelsville Corporation, interviewed seventy-five hundred managers in one hundred and nine different countries. Although his interviews did not include ethics as a subject, he found many managers who wanted to talk about their desire to do good. There was a kind of noble aspiration which sought expression.

There was not much conversation about this in public, for managers are as shy to speak openly about ethics as most people blush to mention God.

Ethical Capability

What does come out in interviews, autobiographies and research studies is the obvious capability of executives for ethical conduct. As Alfred T. Sloan wrote of his many years with General Motors, a group could make policy, but only an individual can administer policy. Or as Luther Hodges, former Secretary of Commerce, said at a conference on ethics and business, "This matter of moral and ethical behavior in business or in government goes back finally to a personal situation." [2]

Suppose we believe that a manager does have the capacity for moral decision in his organization, would he usually be motivated to act in an ethical manner? How would he know what is the right thing to do in the complexity of large-scale organizations?

On the first of these questions we can make some distinctions between routine operation and the times that try men's souls. When there is no great stress for a distinctive decision, the motivation of a manager is unnecessary. He has only to follow the company policy.

Top Men Have Character

But when there is a change of opinion or a call for risky decisions, we discover who has character and why he succeeds. In David Halberstam's *The Best and the Brightest*, there is a page from the diary of Chester Bowles after the

---

[2] *The Ethics of Business*, p. 44.

Bay of Pigs fiasco. The great concern of Mr. Bowles was for a lack of conviction on what was right and wrong among leaders in the administration. He noted that anyone in public life with strong convictions would have a very great advantage in time of strain, for his instincts would be clear and immediate. He would have an abiding conviction that one direction was right and another was wrong. Without a framework of morality, Mr. Bowles saw men who added up pluses and minuses on questions and came to some mental decision. Under normal conditions this pragmatic approach would have succeeded. But when there was a deep challenge to the basic principles of the life of an individual or a nation, even the most brilliant pragmatist failed.

But how can men of conviction be sure they are right? Ethics are often illusive and extremely difficult to pin down. There are many ramifications to any decision, some of which will hurt one person and help another. As I will try to show throughout this book, *there is no one best decision to be made under the circumstances of modern life, but there are some principles that can guide us under any circumstances.*

As Harland Cleveland wrote in Leonard Sayles' *Individualism and Big Business:* "The complexity of modern society and the omnipresence of large-scale organizations not only provide an opportunity for the fullest development of the responsible self; they actually place a premium on the exercise of a greater measure of personal responsibility by more people than ever before." [3]

Don't Trust Your "Heart"

An executive cannot always be sure that he is right be-

---

[3] *Individualism and Big Business,* p. 16.

cause his heart tells him so. But he can increase his ability to recognize moral problems and know the ethical guidelines that have guided men since the beginning of Western civilization. Without this awareness, he is not a good manager, for he will not recognize a social atmosphere in his firm which is psychologically destructive to his members.

An executive may wonder if he has the necessary qualifications for "moral awareness." Who has such purity of heart that he always knows how to will the right thing? Actually, ethical decision making is as much a matter of the head as it is of the heart. The moral influence of a manager depends not only on how conscientious he is in consulting his conscience and following moral precepts, but also on his personal perception and interpretation of his environment. The moral theologians of past generations called this perception of the environment "prudence." It was the ability to see things steady and as a whole. If a man knew what was really going on, he was well-qualified to make a moral decision. If he did not perceive realistically, then the best of his intentions would lead to disaster, which was by definition unethical.

How Does a Man Make Up His Mind?

My concern is with the relation of the head to the heart in decision making. Just how does a man make up his mind about the personal issues that confirm or destroy his character? What are the peculiar problems of these decisions for a responsible leader in a complex organization? *Primary questions for an individual executive are the ancient virtues that have endured: realistic perception (prudence), judicious judgment, integrity under attack (fortitude), self-control (temperance). These cardinal vir-*

tues of character are the pillars of an ethical organization.

Why? Because every industry and every organization develops its own way of doing things, its own climate of judgment about what is acceptable and unacceptable. The major influence upon that moral climate is the man at the top. Find an ethical boss, and you will live in a company with integrity.

1
The Moral Demand Curve

Executive morality is like a demand curve with corporate power on one axis and personal concern on the other. The demand is for a critical path from a manager's office into the attitudes and actions of every employee.

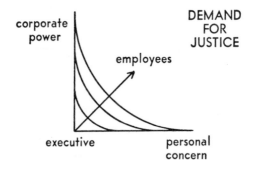

Ethical Efficiency

The manager is not only responsible for the direction that ethics will take in his program, he is also held accountable for the marginal returns on morality. That is, when will additional emphasis upon the rights of an individual add to the costs of the group, and when will corporate strength be increased by individual consideration?

This question of ethical efficiency is posed between employees, between managers, and between employees and managers. Each of these forces is significant for the moral direction of all the others. Raymond Baumhart's study of 1,700 readers of the *Harvard Business Review* showed the most important ethical influence to be a man's equals in the company, followed by the ethical climate of the industry, formal company policy, and the behavior of a man's superiors. Least important was his own personal code of behavior.[1]

The concern of this book is for the weakest factor in ethical efficiency, your own code of behavior. To increase your effectiveness as a moral manager, we will develop the five questions that came out of seminars with senior executives,[2] their wives, and Junior Chamber of Commerce leaders:

- **What kind of a person am I?**
- **To whom am I responsible?**
- **What are the ways and means to achieve moral objectives?**

[1] Raymond Baumhart, "How Ethical Are Businessmen?" *Harvard Business Review*, July-August, 1961.

[2] I am especially grateful for the contributions that senior executives made to the idea in this book through their meetings with me at Northside Drive Baptist Church, Atlanta, Georgia, in the spring of 1974: Bob Guyton, John Humphries, John McIntyre, Frank Nichols, George Smith, Jim Williams.

- **Can I live with the consequences?**
- **What *do* I live for?**

These are guideposts for good decisions. They enable us to do two things: *(1) to define our own objectives for life, and (2) implement these objectives in ways that will maximize their use by others as well.*

As we ask these questions, we discover our perspective, our standpoint on the relation of ethics to our associations. We see our personal preferences for power versus concern for individuals. We measure our willingness to move down the critical path from private moral opinion to executive decisions that influence peers and employees.

The purpose of these questions is not to make you a moral judge over other men, but to increase your awareness of a dimension of executive decision making in which every manager is involved. As Manley Jones argued in *Executive Decision Making,* ethics are inevitable. The higher a man's position in the company hierarchy, the more value premises he must consider. You have to make general estimates of what is good for the company and employees and society because there are not enough facts for a reliable technical forecast, or the externals are imponderable, or the staff recommends many viable alternatives. What do you choose? How? And why?

Chester Barnard summed up the problem in his classic, *Functions of the Executive.* Moral creativeness is the distinguishing mark of executive responsibility. It is the ability to find an ethical basis that others will agree to for the solution of personal and organizational conflicts. Your sincerity, honesty, and personal conviction lead associates to the accomplishments beyond their immediate desires. This process begins in your own ability to transcend your own impulses and work for goals beyond yourself—and your company. Your character is the basis of corporate ethical efficiency.

The Moral Preferences of Managers

A moral demand curve is the product of individual preference and corporate requirements. The question is, what are you willing to pay in terms of risks for the ethics that you prefer? To answer that question, we need to know where we are on the power-personal concern axis. This is the problem of balance. We also need to know how far we have moved from personal conviction toward implementation of ethical decisions with employees and other managers—and the directors or stockholders. This is the problem of motivation.

We can measure our preferences in terms of balance and motivation with an adaptation of the Blake-Mouton grid on leadership styles.[3] We add to our moral demand curve the numbers that correspond to the dominant types of management described by Blake and Mouton:

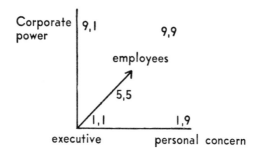

---

[3] R. R. Blake and Jane S. Mouton, *The Managerial Grid* (Houston: Gulf Publishing Co., 1964).

9,1 The Rigid Rule-setter

In the days of the "robber barons," business enterprise and the ethics of love seemed to be irreconcilable. Business was identified with profit and ethics with a denial of self-interest.

The 9,1 executive, who places corporate power first, has two ethical concerns. He warns against greed and covetousness in himself and others. His central question is, "Is it sinful to save?" It is a preoccupation that goes back to J. R. Marriott's *Treatise on Wealth and Life,* 1923, when economics was defined as the science of wealth.

The rigid moralist doesn't break any existing rules in his rush for power, but, as has been said of John D. Rockefeller, Sr., many laws had to be enacted *after* he had done something. The most common moral solution to the overbalancing of power and profit in the nineteenth century was a splurge of good works during the declining days of the successful entrepreneur.

In the last half of the twentieth century, a corporate manager has had to solve the problem of power in a different way. As Frank Abrams of the board of Standard Oil noted in *Fortune,* the job of management is to work out a balance among the claims of various interested groups. The professional executive must balance the demands of stockholders, workers, and consumers. The ethical demand is for prudence more than control of greed, for just decisions among many rather than restraint of rapacity by one owner.

But the second concern of the old-style, power-oriented executive remains. That is judgment of self and others by rigid codes of conduct. Often, these codes apply only to personal or family relations, not to business practices. When reformers asked Mrs. John D. Rockefeller, Sr., how her husband could teach a Sunday school class one day and ruin competitors with railroad rebates on Monday, she replied that Mr. Rockefeller kept religion and business in separate, watertight compartments.

The 9,1 moralist has special compartments for religion, social relations, family obligations, business associations. The only connection between these is a system of authority. In each of these parts of life, there is some central control, some principal or person who makes rules and sees to reward and punishment. Tight control is considered necessary because the rigid moralist believes that the world is out to get him. To be safe, he must test everyone by sure standards of conduct or belief. Those who pass are expected to join him in upholding the rules. Those who fail are held in contempt, and at arms' length.

Rules help the 9,1 moralist keep his hostility under control. Any relaxation is a concern to him; he thinks that other people are more hostile than he is and must be kept within bounds by rigid authority. He believes that corporate power is essential for the survival of civilization, morality, and the corporation.

1,9 The Impulsive Sentimentalist

Horrified by the autocratic and judgmental ways of the 9,1 moralist, other managers equate morality with kind and loving attitudes. They accept the conclusion of Chris Argyris in *Personality and Organization* that the structure of the average business organization is detrimental to personal values. Authoritarianism by executives is considered to be a detriment to self-realization among employees. It fosters dependency and a pretense at conformity.

The 1,9 moralist is "person-centered." Actually, he

screens out some attributes of a mature personality, such as the bravery that opposes injustice or the realism that decides between moral compromise and adjustment to group requirements for work or society. These are neglected in favor of the "affiliation" motive in people, the desire to be liked, to get along, to be part of a big family with low commitment and many laughs.

Ethics are equated with good feelings about other people. To be unethical is to require people to do things that they don't really want to do. In a 1,9 office, each person "does his own thing." Discipline is looked down on as a sign that some executives have a neurotic need for control.

When the 1,9 executive gets in a tight place, where discipline or direction is necessary, he thinks he is moral if he makes some self-sacrifice, such as taking all the blame or backing down on a previous decision. If conflict erupts between employees or peers, he looks impulsively for some quick solution; he does not want to stand the tension of different points of view, even though these must be openly considered before any lasting and realistic solution can be found.

The weakness of the 1,9 position was exposed by Chester Barnard when he wrote that a successful executive has the personal strength to consider all the elements of a problem at one time. Weaker executives see only a part of the issue before them and make premature or incomplete decisions.[4] This incomplete solution sounds ethical to the 1,9 sentimentalist.

1,1 The Complacent Believer

A 1,9 manager is most comfortable in the presence of many 1,1 associates. These complacent persons "make no

---

[4] Chester Barnard, *Functions of the Executive,* p. 235.

waves." Almost anything is OK, so long as the 1,1 doesn't get in trouble because of it.

In contrast to the rule-setter and the sentimentalist, the complacent believer is not uptight about rules, either for or against them. He is the psychologist's "yes-sayer," who gives the church—and the company—such low scores for moral consistency. Why? Because the yes-sayer is agreeable to any question that seems to be socially desirable. When he is asked if he believes in God, he answers "yes." If there is a question on church attendance leading to successful business contacts, he also checks "yes." The only "no's" are about minority races attending his church or sitting in the executive suite. That is not socially desirable, so he's against it.

The 1,1 moralist is a believer—in almost anything. In a management meeting, and in most social gatherings, he buys everybody's ideas—and contributes none of his own. Consequently, he can't be blamed for anything. This is where his moral weakness begins to show. When the boss wants to know why a stupid mistake was made, the 1,1 manager will realistically blame subordinates, because *he* doesn't make decisions. This unwillingness to assume responsibility seems the comfortable thing to do, but brings him under the most severe ethical criticism that we can make. He is unwilling to be identified, to take his share of the load, to state what he believes and stand up for it. To be uncommitted is to be ethically incompetent. He refuses to balance corporate power and personal concern by staying on the bottom, hopefully unrecognized. He forfeits the trust and respect that is due a responsible executive.[5]

---

[5] In *Men, Management and Morality* Robert Golembiewski recommends five activities that earn trust and respect: (1) setting goals with others, (2) defining policy limits on behavior appropriate for

5,5 The Earnest Traditionalist

Right in the middle of the grid is the 5,5 moralist. He really tries to balance concern for people with organizational purposes. His motivation is above that of the complacent believer. All he asks is that someone show him the way. What does the boss say? Is there a ruling in company policy? Who has faced this problem before, and what did they do? Where is this covered in some book of instructions?

The 5,5 moralist combines traits of 9,1 and 1,9 with no attempt at integration. On the one hand, he lives by the rules, but he does not enforce them as *his* regulations. He lacks the force and direction of the rigid rule-setter who has made a commitment to save the company, or his family, or himself from sin. He wants everybody to conform, because that's the best way to get by.

At the same time, the 5,5 moralist is person-centered in his willingness to listen to the opinions of others. When they don't agree with the precedent or tradition that he upholds, he tries persuasion and avoids any direct confrontation. If pushed to make a decision, he'll move toward 9,1 authority rather than retreat into 1,9 sentimentality.

The earnest traditionalist is encouraged by the speeches of business leaders who say that righteous living brings financial rewards. He is disturbed by political or religious spokesmen for any change that clashes his commitment to God-business-family-culture. Those in authority should not raise such questions!

Although the 5,5 moralist is a pleasant and wholesome person, his ethics are swayed by superiors and by colleagues.

---

the goals, (3) checking progress and isolating problems, (4) offering advice and services, (5) relieving subordinates who cannot effectively reach these goals (pp. 261-262).

As *Harvard Business Review* readers showed Raymond Baumhart, there are numerous unethical practices in industry, and a man is often influenced by the ethics of his boss. The best solution to ethical activity is a well-defined *personal* code.

Lawrence Appley saw this personal conviction as the major difference between a mediocre manager and an inspiring executive. A mature executive has a mind that is trained to change when new truth makes change appropriate. The earnest traditionalist needs the question of Mr. Appley in *Values in Management,* "What is different because we have passed through this world"? [6]

9,9 The Realistic Idealist

A 9,9 leader consistently trains others to maximize the marginal returns on morality, to know when additional emphasis on individual rights will benefit corporate growth and when the exercise of corporate power will increase the satisfactions of individuals.

To achieve moral optimality, a manager must combine realism with idealism. He and his associates look clearly at their resources and the alternatives that are open to them. At the same time, they ask: "What *ought* to be?" The team is trained in bifocal vision, to see what is, along with what ought to be.

The adjustment of bifocal vision is an essential talent for a 9,9 moralist. This may mean some conflict as varying viewpoints are brought together. The objective is resolution through a hard look at the facts and a sensitive analysis of feelings. This distinguishes the realistic idealist from the 9,1

---

[6] Lawrence Appley, *Values in Management,* p. 44.

approach to conflict, which is to stop it with an order; the 1,9 attempt to be so subjective that the objective is lost; the 1,1 shrug of the shoulders; and the 5,5 search for somebody else's way of handling it.

A creative leader shares moral decision making with many members of the organization, but he still provides direction and discipline on a more consistent basis than he would expect of any subordinate.

How can an idealist expect so much of himself and still be realistic? His secret is an ability to harness self-interest in a creative way. He has achieved the satisfactions of financial security, corporate recognition, and personal identification as a leader. What he now seeks is an opportunity to make a contribution beyond self or business, to aid community and individual development. He feels secure in the part he has played in the professional and personal development of associates. He has seen evidence of Harland Cleveland's conclusion that "large-scale organizations not only provide an opportunity for the fullest development of the responsible self; they actually place a premium on the exercise of a greater measure of personal responsibility by more people than ever before." [7]

Personal Inputs For Moral Returns

We measure the moral output of an executive by the production of justice in relationships between employer and employee, between employees, and between managers and society. Justice is a product of power and personal concern. It is love in action, a bringing together of person and position for mutual benefit.

---

[7] Leonard R. Sayles, *Individualism and Big Business* (New York: McGraw-Hill, 1963) p. 16.

What are the resources with which an executive balances power-concern and moves morality beyond the private opinions of a manager into the fabric of public decisions in his organization?

The basic input is *character*. Each of the classic definitions of character can increase preferences for ethical relationships and establish a productive critical path of moral choices. The vectors of "cardinal virtues" move on a managerial grid as follows:

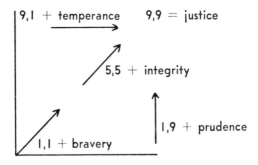

9,1 + temperance

If the rigid rule-setter could see himself as others see him, he could make an excellent contribution to the moral climate of a company. He has convictions and the will to put them into action, but he is narrow-minded and rigid in implementation! He needs to ask himself and others: "What kind of man am I?" so that he can relax some of his rigidities, broaden his perspectives.

The ancient remedy for a closed-minded person was *temperance,* the ability to see all the elements in a decision, including one's own involvement. When we know how we are involved, and recognize the viewpoints of others, rigidity is reduced and rules are related to human potentialities and preferences.

This vector of personal insight and social sensitivity will be discussed in the next chapter, "What happens when I'm involved?" The questions of temperance are:

- **What's in this decision for me?**
- **Should I show how I really feel?**
- **Can I see myself in action?**
- **Will I listen when I'm attacked?**

1,9 + Prudence

The impulsive sentimentalist needs to know what is really going on. If he could really grasp the situation and ask "Just how responsible am I in the midst of all these conflicting forces?" he could be a gracious and humane addition to any conference table.

But the sentimentalist makes decisions on the basis of his perception of ideals, one of which is to reduce tension as quickly as possible! He is more anxious than accurate. The antidote for impulsiveness is the classic virtue of prudence. It is the ability to form a right judgment concerning individual acts exactly as they ought to be done here and now. It is a talent of seeing steadily and broadly. The prudent manager begins with deliberation and ends in a sound decision.

The practice of prudence involves these questions:

- **Am I honest with myself? (Do *I* know what's going on?)**
- **Am I frank with others? (Do I measure my perception by that of others?)**
- **Why do I take this action? (What do I expect to happen?)**
- **Should I act now? (How's my timing?)**

The impulsive sentimentalist has a sense of moral imperative. He is ready to act on behalf of others or ideals beyond them. He needs to develop some tolerance for uncertainty and patience to see what is really going on. This is the exercise of prudence which we will introduce in chapter four with the question: "When and how do I act?"

1,1 + Bravery

The complacent believer has all the right ideas, but his heart is not in any of them. If we could just bring head and heart together!

The 1,1 moralist needs fortitude. This is a willingness to take deliberate action with knowledge of consequences, and face those consequences without reversing the decision. It's cheerfulness in the midst of pressure, consistency despite conflicting opinions. As some managers said, "You live with the decision. You seek opinions, make a judgment, stick your neck out and keep it there." These executives judged the effectiveness of decision making by this question: "Will it last?"

A brave leader is patient in explaining what has been decided and resolute in dealing with opposition. He finds satisfaction in standing fast, seeing the way through a difficult period of transition. This is possible when he asks himself and others some questions:

- **Have I counted the cost? (Did I look ahead?)**
- **Will I be rewarded? (What do I expect to happen that will bring me satisfaction—perhaps fortitude will be its own reward?)**
- **Am I willing to recheck the ground we have covered? (Do I listen to feedback and make adjustments?)**
- **Can I be cheerful? (Am I assured that the goal of this decision goes beyond my own comfort at the moment?)**

We move the complacent believer ahead by asking him about the consequences of his beliefs. If he is agreeable with our ideas, what are the consequences for him? This is our direction in chapter five.

5,5 + Integrity

The earnest traditionalist is willing to face consequences, so long as someone else in authority has already done the same. He'll keep the right balance between corporate power and personal concern if he doesn't have to make the decision on his own.

We turn this proper person into a pioneer when we stir up his desire to live for something more than security on the job. We ask him a very personal question, "What do you live for?" Hopefully this will measure his emotional maturity.

- **Am I still concerned about conformity? (That's the problem of a delayed adolescent!)**
- **Does the masculine ego really matter? (The issue should be settled very early in marriage.)**
- **Is "personality" the way to get ahead? (Can you really carry that college pep into middle age?)**
- **Do I judge everyone by his success in private enterprise? (Does property really count more than personal relationships?)**

The question on which a 5,5 moralist stumbles is a measure of his maturity. The further he can go with the questions, the closer he is to the self-actualization of a 9,9 leader.

9,9 The Creative Balance

Mature morality has the qualities of precision, balance, force, and appropriateness. Precision is an awareness of what we stand for, an ability to articulate for a group of people the values that should guide them in a decision. Balance is a talent for maximizing individual and corporate goals and resolving conflicts between the two. Force is a sense of moral imperative that moves a leader and his group toward the best solution to management problems. Appropriateness is a sense of timing, not just in terms of deadlines to be met, but also in terms of psychological readiness for decision. Timing also involves our knowledge of what is possible. Is this a "teachable" moment for the staff, a time for resolution of issues, because the resources are now available for us to act if we want to?

The combination of these qualities is justice. We practice this virtue in our answers to such questions as:

- **Do I hold the balances steady? (Am I a stable leader who makes his own position clear?)**
- **Do I know the demands that I must meet? (For what decisions am I really obligated?)**
- **Are my feelings under control in promotions and firings? (Can I restore balance and reward initiative?)**

Effective personal ethics requires the exercise of judgment on behalf of others and a spirit of faith and hope when the judgment is upon us. Our personal commitments are most clearly revealed in our attitudes and actions after *we* seem to experience injustice. Can we still believe in a good world when powerful people act against us? The answer to that question will be seen in a case study in our final chapter. We will also look at the requirements for a creative ethical balance in chapter 3, "What are my responsibilities?"

What's in the Little Black Box?

The spiritual qualities of an administrator are measured by his answers to these questions. They tell us what an executive believes in, what he will fight for. Ultimately, as O. A. Ohmann wrote in his classic article on sky-hooks, the successful executive shows that he believes in a God who created the world and holds men ultimately responsible to Him.

The assertion of Ohmann leads us into the depths of personal convictions, which may be so difficult to fathom that they are like the "little black box" of a cybernetic decision making model:

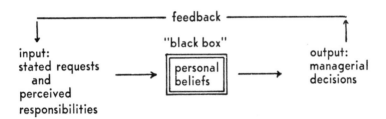

The questions in this volume are designed to shed light into the "little black box," to help you define your values, order your personal priorities, sort out your moral satisfactions in life. What do you really find worthwhile about yourself and your associates? What do you want them to remember about you that will last?

2
What Happens When I'm Involved?

There seems to be a contradiction in the title question. How can an executive be personally involved in a decision and still be ethical? "Personal involvement" sounds like "conflict of interest." Surely any experienced executive would divest himself of shares in a supplier agency when he becomes a production or purchasing vice-president!

But most questions about involvement are not so precise. The subtle influences of pride, position, personal pique are at work. How can we look objectively at a proposal when it will benefit a rival? What are we going to say in the evaluation of a marginally-competent employee who reminds us that he and our father were good friends? Can we think together in a director's meeting with men who make more money than we do, but are no more competent in our eyes? Will we vote in a civic planning session for programs that give more prominence to a business competitor? We could have done the job, but he has the right connections.

The wives of senior executives are especially sensitive to this part of leadership. It is natural, because they are most concerned about their husbands as persons and think the most about the human side of management. Wives, and employees, are impressed by the self-forgetfulness of an executive as he resolves problems which *could* have much to do with his own position, status, and security. The executive with this quality is one who really believes that other people are important. This is conveyed in all of his dealings with them, in his conversations about decisions with others, including the wife. Although he is vitally involved in numerous decisions, he does not make himself the center of everything or secretly seek to strengthen his own position when all alternatives are being considered.

The women are really describing one of the cardinal virtues, temperance. This is the ability to preserve yourself through selflessness. It is the development of an inner discipline that restrains your self-assertion or the immediate fulfillment of your own desires.

When I talk with senior executives, they agree with their wives, but have more emphasis upon another quality of temperance. This is the talent of disposing various parts of a problem in one unified and ordered whole. This is really a consequence of what the wives have already described about them. *That is, the senior member of a management team can look at the total picture because he is not blinded by envy of another manager, pride in his office, or vengeance towards those who have disagreed with him.*

Does this sound like a contradiction? On the one hand, the executive is said to be moral when he becomes personally involved in decisions. On the other hand, wives and employees say that he is a man of character when he does not think about himself in these decisions. How is this to be possible in one person?

What's in It for You?

Selfishness is subdued when there is a reward for self-forgetfulness. Psychologically, a character trait will endure when it is reinforced. What we want to do is to find a "profit motive" for humility and generosity toward others.

How can an executive get anything out of unselfishness? The answer lies in his scale of values. The higher his sense of satisfaction, the less his concern to get things at the expense of other people.

Senior executives referred to a "hierarchy of values" when they discussed the question of gifts to managers. They cited examples of inexperienced managers who were so influenced by free trips by a client that they made errors in judgment. Some companies avoid this by advising executives to report all gifts over $10.00. Some say that no gifts may be accepted over $25.00. But what about trips and social invitations? The senior executives concluded that distortions of judgment were more of a concern to younger managers who had not yet achieved a sizable salary or a sense of experience in judgment. The senior executive has enough discretionary income to take trips on his own. He is not dazzled by the extras offered to a young manager who has never sat at the top. Consequently, a senior executive may acknowledge friendships by keeping close to customers and suppliers through an active social life. Golf games, dinners, trips are acceptable means of showing how much he values the people who keep him in business.

What are the senior executives saying? Are they putting

themselves morally above the temptations of other men? No, they are applying a psychological rule that was developed by Abraham Maslow. Dr. Maslow taught that certain basic needs in life must be met before higher ones can be enjoyed. That is, we must first meet our needs for food, shelter, safety. Then we can appreciate a sense of belonging and affiliation with others. Most persons are satisfied if they can reach such a level of social security. Some persons move on to satisfaction in a specific accomplishment. A sense of service to others can be their chief aim in life. A few move to a fifth stage, where creativity is all important. These are "the self-actualized" persons, who are not moved by appeals of money, sex, social advancement. They have already achieved the desired satisfactions in those areas and are now thinking of what they can generate as a unique contribution to life.

A senior executive is usually satisfied with the financial gains and the social recognition that is offered to him. This is not the level of advancement that challenges him. The influence that moves him is quite subtle. It appears in the visits by men of high office who call upon him to lead some community campaign, or the sharing of confidences in him by some respected member of the board of directors.

The junior executive is still years away from that level of influence. He is just struggling out of the problems of financial security and into the level of personal achievement. Since his needs for recognition and for financial rewards have

not yet been met, he can be influenced by gifts and important visitors.

A kind of stair-step morality is possible in most companies. With years of advancement, an executive can achieve financial satisfaction and mutual recognition. This much the organization can do for him. The crucial question is, will his quality of need go up with economic and social gratification? Will he keep on looking for something more than these? The young men who are going to make it are those who show some desire for creativeness or contribution to society, who have a sense of uniqueness from the beginning of their careers.

A young executive on the way up has already figured out the reasons for selflessness. Here are some answers from JC's:

"You've got to accept criticism without being defensive. Why not learn from everybody? If I listen, I learn something about myself. So I appreciate what the other guy is doing for me."

"Let the boss know that you're thinking through problems *with* him. Sometimes he says you're wrong, and sometimes you criticize his solutions. But you look at the issues for the good of the company, not just to build up yourself or to put somebody else down."

"Get your own head in order. Have confidence

in yourself and in the organization. Then you don't think about yourself all the time. You know that you'll go on up if you do the job."

"Greed? Sure I would like to have a little more, and you're right, I do see some guys getting a little ahead of me. If it's for the good of the company, why, OK, they deserve it. Why eat my guts out over that? If I learn from them, I'll go on up with them. If they haven't got it—you know, just brown-nosing—then they won't be there long."

What are these young men saying about themselves? First, they have confidence in themselves. They believe they can produce. If they listen and learn, experience will bring them quickly to the top.

Second, they know how to look ahead. They don't spin their wheels in useless resentment about some temporary pass-over in favor of another. They learn from the favored one and from anyone else so that they will be wiser and more eligible for promotion.

Third, they really enjoy the organization and its aims. They believe in what they're doing, and that is a stronger motivation than promotion. Unless the promotion is for the good of the group, they feel uneasy. It would sound too much like pushing for self alone.

Fourth, they believe that the senior executives share their aims and observe their efforts. The result will be a reward for competent and cooperative service.

In summary, these men know themselves pretty well,

and they gain strength from what they know. To put it in a paradox, they have a centered self, but they're not self-centered. The junior executive who "has his head together" is a centered self. That is, he has an executive center for self-management, a set of ideals to guide him, and a determination to order his emotions to achieve those goals over a period of years.

In contrast, the self-centered executive is not quite sure of what's inside him, and he doesn't find lasting satisfaction in what he does achieve. His appetite for recognition is enormous, but he draws no lasting strength from that which he receives. Why? For one thing, he sets such impossible, unrealistic goals that nothing really pleases him. Like the classic alcoholic, he has a big ego. He is king in his own mind. When others treat him only as an equal, or less, he burns inwardly with resentment.

Another problem for the big ego is interpersonal. This person draws insatiably from others, and pays attention only to those who can feed his ego. What happens to a staff or a company with that kind of ego-drain? This flawed executive consistently *defeats one of the prime requisites of management, that the manager be able to support and feed those who work with him and that they recognize his attention as appreciation of what they contribute to the total organization.*

Our initial question was "What's in it for you?" We have seen that the executives who are really *in* the organization are gaining satisfaction from cooperative endeavor and future attainment. This is possible when he knows who he is and what he wants. When his needs correspond to the greater good of those about him, everybody wins.

Should Your Feelings Show?

But how are you going to know that *your* satisfactions are going to help others? There has to be some sharing of ideas and goals before you'll really know. This means showing something of your inner self, letting others know what really makes you tick.

The question, "What does the boss really think?" is so intriguing that one business magazine has an inside story on some executive every few issues. We all want to know what moves the man who is at the top.

But as we move toward the top, we think we must be so tough that our feelings are hidden, more and more. An executive told Fernando Bartolome:

"I have difficulties expressing feelings. It could have something to do with my job as head of an R&D team. When you have this kind of job, you cannot trust people; you have to check that their thoughts and actions are right." [1]

In interviews with forty younger executives and their wives, Mr. Bartolome found their difficulty in showing tenderness toward the persons they love and in acknowledging any need for others. The men felt that toughness brought success, that a display of how you felt would cause loss of respect.

Yet the executives realized that their success depended in large part on the way they got along with other people, on their ability to be a live human being. They are

[1] Fernando Bartolome, "Executives as Human Beings," *Harvard Business Review,* November-December, 1972, p. 63.

caught in the bind that a middle manager brought to me about his senior executive:

> **"I like Al [senior executive] for what he's doing for our organization, so far as having good ideas and all that—but, man, you can't get anything out of him as a person! I mean, when I take him a problem that is tearing my guts out, he just looks concerned and says he hopes I can work it out. If it's technical, he makes some comment, but if it's like the last one—when I really needed to know if I was adequate for the job—after all the backing and filling and bull I got from the [expletive deleted] plant staff last month during our reorganization, I was really shook up. I didn't know if I could make it—and if I was going in the direction that he would really support. Well, I told him how I felt, and he told me to do what I thought best, and then he just sat there and kinda smiled. I waited for a minute, and when he didn't say anything else, I just got up and nodded to him and walked out. He never said a word!"**

I would imagine that the chief executive of that company will soon be transferred. His plant managers never know where they stand with him. He always shows interest, but he never commits himself emotionally to anyone or any point of view. Who knows what really pleases him? He's opaque.

In contrast, I see the transparency of experienced executives. You can tell what they enjoy and what displeases them. It's usually not an explosive display; it's just a quiet sense of satisfaction in that which you know you like. And, they're secure enough to let it show.

When I asked a group of presidents, vice-presidents, and general managers for the sense of reward they had in their position, several spoke immediately of their satisfactions in seeing younger men grow and produce strong and imaginative programs for a company. They were especially satisfied when this was combined with a sense of civic responsibility and development of the corporation in line with community needs.

The men talked like fathers who were proud of their sons. It did not seem to be the old-fashioned paternalism of those who expected others to follow exactly in their footsteps. Some of the oncoming executives were doing things differently. But the fifty- and sixty-year-old managers were obviously pleased with the successes of those whom they had trained, or to whom they had given opportunity and support. They spoke with enthusiasm; they smiled; their gestures were free and expansive.

The Right Way to Do It

I saw this same enjoyment of other people in the calls of executives from their office. One who had trained hundreds of branch managers was interrupted by a call during my visit. He first kidded his colleague for some statements that had been made at a staff meeting, then listened with interest to whatever was being proposed, asked how he could help, and pledged specific support. I did not mind the interruption in our conversation because I saw the obvious pleasure of this manager in serving someone in whom he had an interest.

Executives' wives attribute much of their husbands' success to the contagious quality of their confidence and enthusiasm for the business. One of the wives said: "Sometimes, when I am waiting for him, I will see one of his sales directors go in for advice on something. I can see that the man is troubled and worried. When he comes out of the office, he looks sure of himself. When I ask Ed [her husband] about it, he will just say that he helped a good man work out a problem. He really believes in the people that work with him, and it doesn't take them but a few minutes to realize that when they talk with him. I am sure that his years of experience help in solving problems. But I also think that he believes so much in what he is doing and the people that are doing it with him, that this gives them the boost that they need to get the job done."

These executives are in contact with their own feelings about their work, and they really enjoy what they feel. Furthermore, they can be open enough with others for this to be contagious.

But just how open should you be? We'll consider the question in more detail in another chapter. For the present let's not jump to the conclusion that a moral manager is to show everything he's feeling all the time. Also, let's acknowledge the distinction between the competent executive who is secure enough to show concern for others and the incompetent executive who flies into a rage when he does not know how to handle some situation. Wives learn from their husbands, from other employees, and from their own observation that the expression of feelings by some executives is only a sign of their anxiety. A wife said: "When we were in Central City, and Ted was a district manager, I worked in the bookkeeping section. I saw how the general manager behaved with people who came to him for answers. He was gruff and rough. He didn't listen; he directed. Ted and I would talk this over, and I listened to what other people said, also. It seemed that this man had been elevated to a responsibility that he could not handle. That's why he would stomp around the office and be short-tempered with everyone. He seemed to think that he was supposed to have all of the answers because of his position. He wasn't like Ted. Ted would listen to what others had to say, and he respected their solutions to problems. What makes some of these men so different?"

The difference is in feeling *with* people rather than feeling above them. The competent executive is not afraid to show concern, surprise, joy, anger. All of these emotions help people know where we stand and where they stand with us. If we mask our emotions, as I often do, then people wonder what I am thinking. They say: "We are never quite sure of what you are going to do."

What can you do with such a question? One thing I try is more inquiry. I ask people what they think of my actions and what they believe that I have left out of some explanation. This is often an opportunity to clarify my position. It also encourages me to show how I am feeling as I move toward a decision.

Wives have another question to raise about an executive's feelings. If a man is personally involved in what happens at work, how can he turn off his emotions when he gets home? Wives try to solve this problem by acting as careful listeners, sympathetic companions, someone that he can talk to in confidence. The wives believe that a man is basically the same at home and at the office, but they do think that he can become a little more detached from personnel decisions when he talks about these problems at home. Then he is more able to make a decision objectively, and when he has to tell it like it is to an employee, he won't let his personal feelings get in the way.

The higher a man goes in the business, the worse this problem seems to become. Junior executives tell me that they seldom stay awake at night worrying about a decision. One said: "I can see the v.p. doing this—millions of dollars and the careers of many people may be riding on what he decides. But me—well, it will be some years before any long-term decisions depend on what *I* think about at night."

What does a senior executive do with his worry about work, his concern for the right decision? This is more than being technically correct. It's a problem of helping rather than hurting certain people. One of our solutions has been to suggest more sharing with colleagues. Responsible members of a management team will carry a burden with us, if we are willing to show what we're going through. That makes us more vulnerable, of course, but if we trust them, they may respond with faith, honesty, and support.

Can You See Yourself In Action?

There's another advantage to consider. If we begin to tell what's happening to us, we'll become more aware of ourselves in the process of depending on others. How does this happen?

Sales Manager: "I'd like for this sales meeting to be a little different. Last week some of you told me that I make all the decisions. That's right, and it's getting a little heavy, carrying all that. I think the market is so screwy now that nobody can predict what kind of houses the public will buy. So we need to go beyond guesswork by one person. OK. [Several staff persons nod in affirmation.] So I've asked George if he would form a team to check out buyer preferences among new families moving into town. You tell 'em, George."

George: "We're going to ask some new people in town just what kind of house they want. And we thought it would be a good idea to get the names of some close friends from those who buy our houses and ask for their preferences."

Manager: "I'd like for George and, ah, maybe you, Ed, and Rachael. We need a woman to help kick this off."

George: "Ah, Ralph [manager], I though we were going to talk about this some and then decide who would like to do it."

Manager: "Sure, sure, that's what we're doing. (Looks puzzled for a moment, then smiles and says,) Now the first thing I want you to do, Ed—"

Ed: "Is George right? I mean, do we have a choice?"

Manager: "I just said so, didn't I?"

Ed: "Then what choice do I have? I mean, I'll do what you say, but did you mean for us to talk about this first, get the idea, and then—"

Manager: "Sure, sure, you get the idea, don't you?"

Ed: "Well, yeah, like you have decided, and

so now we'll move ahead. Ah, that's OK, but I was just puzzled."

Manager: "Say George, what [expletive deleted] is going on here? I thought we'd get lots of cooperation."

George: "Maybe we will, if we back up and let everybody in the act."

Manager: Well, aren't they?" [Waves arm in sweeping gesture.]

Rachael: "You *put* me in the act. You're the boss. I'll go along."

Manager: "Do you *want* to?"

Rachael: "If you had asked who liked the idea, I would probably have volunteered."

Manager: "Well, I just thought you'd be a natural for this."

Rachael: "Yes, but you started out saying that we'd talk and get the idea, and then, I thought, we'd see who wanted to do this."

Manager: "Well, OK, we'll do it that way. Any suggestions?"

George: "I think you named good people, but I'd wait a minute and see who thinks what of the idea."

After several meetings like this, the staff was convinced that the general manager really wanted them with him in the troublesome decisions brought on by a fluctuating buyer market. But they always had to stop him several times to let them help in the decision. Over a period of time, they began to understand each other better:

Manager: "What do you mean, it's just another cut-and-dried decision? I thought we settled that weeks ago. We're getting into these decisions together."

Ed: "OK, Ralph, but each time we have to stop you. I get tired of stepping in front of a freight train."

Manager: "Oh, come on, it's not really that bad. Look, I just got lots of pressure. I need some decisions."

Rachael: "Ed, you know that Ralph will listen if you stand up and say what you think. Like this morning, he wanted to cut the price on K model, and Phyllis and I kept him from doing it, right?"

Manager: "Yeah, that's so. But Ed is right. You do have to put forth some effort to slow me down when I'm under pressure. Otherwise I just whiz ahead."

Later, on their way to another meeting, Ralph asked George, "Say, how am I doing? Are people really speaking up?" George replied, "Yeah, we talked about it some, and there was some fear at first that you'd resent anyone who crossed you and do them in later. But it hasn't happened. I think it will work out OK. You feel better?" Ralph smiled and replied, "Sure do. I don't feel like I'm carrying everything uphill by myself."

Ralph was now beginning to see himself in action. And

he found that it not only helped him with his own staff, it provided wisdom to others up the line. Ralph and the vice-president for sales were together about a month after Ralph had begun to see how fast he moved under pressure. The vice-president said: "Boy, am I glad to get out of that meeting with the president! He had some complaints from some of you guys about the way I shifted advertising money around. You know that's a big job, and Harry [another general manager] was really burned up because I sent money to another region that he thought he should have. I told him the reasons, and he said I should have told him the reasons before I left him high and dry."

Ralph: "You agree?"

V.P.: "Well, yes, but what was I to do?"

Ralph: "Well, you have us together every month. Why not wait until then to move the money, unless you're under pressure to do something at once—are you?"

V.P.: "No, not usually. I guess I could do that. But you know me, when I see what's right, I want to get it done."

Ralph: "I'm the same way. And my staff says that's why I get into trouble with them—like you're getting with Harry."

V.P.: [Grins.] "Yeah, I would say that's where we're alike. You know your mind and don't mess around when you decide."

Ralph: "Well, it caused some mess. I was carrying too much of the load by myself. But I couldn't wait to ask the staff for advice and support. I'd just decide and then push them to *do* it."

V.P.: "Heh, Heh, that's me, too!"

Ralph: "Now they're stopping me and making sure that we all understand what has to be done. Then we share the responsibility."

V.P.: "I'll try it. Draw up a proposal for me."

Ralph: "That may help. But seriously, if you agree that you're like me, you'll have to accept some real checks—we're pretty impulsive under pressure, you know—accustomed to making the decisions."

V.P.: "It's not worth it, taking all that [expletive deleted] from the old man and Harry. Besides, it sounds like a good idea. Then, if a guy takes the money for advertising in his region, we'll ask next month if it did him more good than if the next manager had it. That ought to help. Now people just expect me to hand it out, like I was Santa Claus, and then I don't know if I'm getting results. Am I losing my touch?"

A sure sense of touch comes from the ability to see yourself in action. When you can identify what you are feeling and are in touch with the emotions of others, then you can balance the objective side of a problem with the subjective impact that it will have upon human beings. It is this emotional side of the issue that most often gives rise to questions about ethics. When people say that we were "immoral" in some action, they often mean that we did not take enough time to discuss this with the principals in the drama, or that we showed some lack of concern for what was happening to individuals.

Are You Really Strong Enough?

A periodic reappraisal of who we are in the eyes of our associates will take some courage. Are we really strong enough to listen without being defensive or cutting down the other person? Here is a paradox; the more confident we are in ourselves, the more open we are to opinions from others. The result is a more realistic self-estimate and more security in interpersonal transactions. On the other hand, if we are personally inadequate, we fear any criticism and continually seek to arm ourselves with the dignity of our office, the unanswerable nature of our pronouncements. We see ourselves less and less and become more and more ineffective.

The way out of this vicious circle is to combine courage with high ideals. We have already seen the necessity for an executive to move from one level of need to another. Now we must consider the fortitude with which he presses on toward a higher level.

This part of character development is like resource management. An executive must consider the opportunity cost of self-development. This includes the question of what he will give up. When he is personally involved in a decision, he must give up any traits of unexamined arrogance, self-pity, and impetuous ambition. When he values these less than cooperation, concern, and character, then the marginal utility of morality is worth the cost.

In economic theory we would say the mature manager is continually moving from one level of moral demand to another. Once he has achieved satisfaction in financial security and social significance, he exerts a personal preference for the additional benefits of unique contributions to company and society, a general concern for the welfare of people in his organization and in the community. The level of personal satisfaction is continually rising.

Courage is required to demand and maintain a high level of moral creativeness. Once we have made a decision, we must be willing to say the same thing about it to all groups, whether they agree or not.

A Specific Example

A brave manager takes some risk for what he believes in. The general manager of a small corporation in the South felt required to take some action when a national magazine developed a story on new industries in small towns. This was back in the days of racial change. The corporation was to be featured in this story. Before the writers arrived, the general manager proposed to his associates that the cafeteria be completely integrated. Blacks and whites had been going through the same cafeteria line, but then going to one or the other side of a large room that was separated by a movable partition. Although several supervisors objected, the majority of the management group were favorable to a removal of the partition and a deliberate attempt to seat themselves anywhere in the cafeteria. Afterwards, one of the supervisors said to the general manager: "Joe, that was a neat trick. We will save face with those New Yorkers. Then everybody can go back to the way we were after they leave."

The general manager realized that his gains in civil rights were quite temporary. What could make them more permanent policy? The company had no government contracts, and at that time there was no enforceable anti-discrimination legislation in his state. His wife told him that he had gone far enough. She admired the courage of his convictions, but she feared social ostracism for the children if he went too far.

The general manager called on a close friend who was secretary of the board of directors. The friend advised: "Joe, nothing is going to be permanent until Mr. Taber [Chairman of the Board] signs some kind of agreement. If you can get his signature, the rest of us will go along. You seem to want this integration pretty badly. I don't know whether it's because you are a religious man, or whether you just think that it will be good publicity for the company right now. For myself, I think it's risky, but then we could really be clobbered, like you say, if those reporters got to asking the wrong questions about race. I guess they would have to do that in discussing labor in the South. So go ahead. If the old man signs, I will back you up."

The next day, the general manager drove thirty miles to the major city of the region where Mr. Taber had his office in a bank building. Everything in Mr. Taber's office was exactly as it had been since the general manager had called on him with his father twenty years ago. And Miss Rogow was still his secretary. She greeted "her boy" warmly and took him into Mr. Taber's office with many questions about the wife and children.

Mr. Taber turned his chair around from a rolltop desk and said: "Well, Joe, I am glad to see you. I know that you and the boys at the plant are all happy about this publicity that we are going to get. I would offer you a cigar, but I know that you are very strict about that sort of thing [laughs, picks up cigar, cuts it in half and begins to chew on one end]. I don't smoke either you know. It would be a sin to burn up anything that is that good to chew!"

General Manager: [Who has heard this particular saying at least one hundred and fifty times]: "Thank you, Mr. Taber. We are all very glad about what is going to happen, but I am worried about something that requires your advice and action."

Mr. Taber: "Oh? Speak right up, boy. I am behind you one hundred percent."

General Manager: "I already know from some of the telephone conversations with the magazine writers in New York that they are going to ask questions about race. They have already asked how many blacks we have in managerial positions."

Mr. Taber: "Oh, [expletive deleted] why don't they leave us alone! We know how to work out these kinds of problems ourselves."

General Manager: "Well, sir, I think we have to work it out in such a way that we don't get any black marks in our national connections—

Mr. Taber: "Black marks! Say, that's pretty good. Which blacks are going to do the marking?" [Laughs.]

General Manager: "They will mark us pretty badly if we don't have some fair practice policies in print. We have already taken down the partitions in the cafeteria so that the visitors can see that everybody eats together. But we have got to do something more permanent. We've got to show them a policy statement signed by the Board. At least this is what I think. Now I have to leave this to you."

Mr. Taber: "Now, Joe, you know that I want to do the right thing. Your father and I were on the Board of Stewards [in the Methodist Church] together. I know that you are very serious about this kind of thing. But I just don't think that we ought to go this far right now."

General Manager: "Well, what kind of a Christian witness will we be giving if the magazine says that we are keeping down colored people?"

Mr. Taber: "I know that you are right, but I just don't want to do it. I wasn't raised that way. Why did that blamed magazine have to poke its nose into our state, anyway?"

General Manager: "They think that we are an example of the way in which a company can serve a community. It will be a witness to many people, including some that you and I know. It will strengthen community relationships for us, and it will give us some new national contacts. But you know that it can all blow up in our face if we do not have a good policy on race to show those reporters."

Mr. Taber: "I know, I know. I wish I had thought of this before we agreed to let them come down here. [Expletive deleted], I don't want to sign."

General Manager: "Here's the policy statement. I know that Jim and others on the Board of Directors will sign if you do."

Mr. Taber: "I don't want to look at it. I know what it says. I know what all of them say. Why don't you just go do it?"

General Manager: "It can't be done without your signature. It won't mean anything without your influence. You built the business. You have more money in it than anyone else. You are known as a man of conviction."

Mr. Taber: "Convictions can get you into trouble around here when you make the wrong application. Had you thought about that?"

General Manager: "Yes, and now it is up to you. Are we going to risk some trouble around here or lots of trouble with our national contacts? Which way do you want the company to go in the next few years: local or national?"

Mr. Taber: "How can anybody get out of the kinds of questions that you ask? [Begins to cry.] I am an old man. I built up this company, and we have always been proud of it. Now you are asking me to do something that goes against everything that I stand for."

General Manager: "Does it really go against everything that you stand for—as a Methodist steward?"

Mr. Taber: [Continues to cry]: I know that you are right, [expletive deleted]. I know I've got to do it, but I just don't want to."

> **General Manager:** "Sign it. I hate to see you cry. Sign it and you will stop crying." [Hands pen to Director.]
>
> **Mr. Taber:** [Sniffs]: "This is a terrible thing that you are asking me to do. I never thought that I would have to do it. Where do I sign?" [Signs policy.]
>
> **General Manager:** [Removes paper from Director so that tears will not blot the signature.] "You have done the right thing. I know it's hard to do. Others know this, too. Since you have done this, they will have the courage to sign also."
>
> **Mr. Taber:** "Take the [expletive deleted] thing out of my office and tell everyone of them to sign it, or I'll nail their hides to the wall!"

The General Manager's persistence combined selflessness with personal self-affirmation. On the one hand, he was willing to risk his own personal convenience for the sake of a principle. On the other hand, he pushed the importance of an immediate decision. This was his judgment, his timing. There was, also, a sense of cooperation with those who controlled the business. He wanted them to make the final decision. He had courage in stating his own position, but he did not say that this must be done for him or that he must be backed up on something that he decided without consultation.

The desired combination is courage with conviction, high-mindedness with humility. In the last analysis, we are able to see the whole picture and make a realistic decision because of the way that virtues combine in our own character. When selflessness is combined with bravery, we have a sense of frankness with ourselves and others. We are willing to see exactly who we are and how we relate to others, despite the pain and humiliation that sometimes occurs. When we combine a frank admission of what we want for ourselves with high ideals, then we obtain a consistent system of rewards for ourselves in respect for others, joy at their advancement, compassion and concern for their difficulties. We look realistically at what we have to give up in order to get something that is better.

The combination of virtues will also correct excesses in any one area. For example, the wives of executives were disgusted by the rough and gruff ways of some managers. This was attributed to their misunderstanding of the requirements of their position, or to their personal inadequacies in the position. But we need to say something else about gentleness. It is the right combination of self-assurance with concern for others. The executive who can see himself in action and is satisfied with his observations has a sure sense of personal worth. He is strong enough to be gentle. He can listen, and he can reflect on the opinions of others because he does not think that he is being personally jeopardized.

As we move through this book, we will see other examples of the combination of virtues. When humility is combined with bravery, we are gentle. But when gentleness is not backed up by bravery, the result is a bland personality which really stands for nothing but easy circumstances at any particular moment. When temperance is combined with justice, we can make firm decisions that bring trust and stability to the organization. But when we are "temperant" without a sense of justice, the result is sentimentality. We end up trying to do therapeutic things for inadequate people, which result in injustice to the competent and conscientious members of our organization.

The combination of these virtues is the function of temperance. This is why we are asking "what kind of man are you?" before we talk about some specific characteristics of a moral person. There has to be some executive center of character just as there is a decision maker in a company. We must know what kind of person we are and how we relate to others before we can understand how to be just in our decisions, how to apply policy to specific projects. All of these questions are conditioned by our own temperament and outlook. As Luther Hodges, former Secretary of Commerce, said to a conference on ethics and business, "This matter of moral and ethical behavior in business or in government goes back finally to a personal situation." [5]

---

[5] *The Ethics of Business,* p. 44.

3
To Whom Am I Responsible?

"Middle management is an elephant's graveyard —and I have to bury one this week." The junior executive was not anxious as he said this, but he was intense in seeking an answer to the major question of justice in an organization: "I want to do what is right for this man who has been in the company since I was in high school. How can I move him out of a position in which he no longer operates effectively and still not hurt him? If he stays where he is, he will hurt others. Morale is already low in his section. He knows that he is not really needed, and he is puzzled because he cannot get results. It is time for his performance report, and I must either reduce him to a position that I used to occupy, try to transfer him, or see if he is eligible for early retirement."

To whom was the executive responsible? On the one hand he had to consider the employees who were under an incompetent administrator. He also had to consider the trust placed in him by management and the investments of stockholders. All these persons expected competent leadership and effective production. They held him responsible for the conditions under which this would be possible in his section of the company. On the other hand, he had a sense of responsibility to a loyal, long-term employee. He was about to make a change in the life of another human being. How could he care for this person and also act justly toward others in the organization?

When a group of managers discussed this problem, they brought out the major questions about justice:

> **Mr. Ord:** "It seems to me that we have to start with the individual."
>
> **Mr. Fleishman:** "Which one?"
>
> **Mr. Ord:** "Ah, the 'aging elephant' [general laughter]. I mean, he's got the most to lose. And you can't just run roughshod over a person, especially one with those years of experience in the company."
>
> **Mr. Fleishman:** "I don't think my company, or yours, is supposed to be a hospital. The infirm have to be cared for somewhere else. We have hospital insurance and retirement plans for that. No. I think the first question is, what are the demands on this manager?"
>
> **Leader:** "You mean, to whom is he most responsible?"
>
> **Miss Alva:** "Couldn't he show concern for the man he evaluates and still be fair with the other employees? I believe he'll come out OK if

he'll just act with determination and consideration. But he has to make a decision. What I
despise are men who can't make up their minds!"

Mr. Fleishman: "Wow! Listen to the Women's
Liberator. But seriously, you're right. He has the
responsibility, so he has to do something. It
would be unjust for him to just let it ride. Why?
Well, because he has all those people to consider,
and the owners."

Mr. Ord: [expletive deleted]: "So you're just
going to dump an old man out on the street!"

Mr. Fleishman: "There are many considerate
things he could do, like tell him exactly where
he stands, just how people see him, and then
think about the place where he would still be
effective. Like a position with less responsibility,
or a transfer."

Miss Alva: "I despise that! It's a cop-out. You
don't tell him what's wrong, and you sell him
blind to another department. Then *they* have a
problem. That's real injustice."

Leader: "Ah, one principle seems to be that
the man to be evaluated must hear the truth
about himself—or at—"

Mr. Fleishman: "Or at least be told . . . sometimes they don't hear what you tell them, but we
do owe it to them to say what we're thinking,
and why we're acting."

Leader: "And then negotiate with him for
another placement, with all the cards on the
table?" [Group nods.]

Mr. Ord: "You [nodding at Fleishman] refer

to employees as 'them.' You talk about some sort of dispensing of justice. You look down on them. Like this fellow, who has respect for all he's done for his company? Where is there any concern in what we're saying?"

Miss Alva: "You don't have to separate concern from action. Ah, you know what I'm saying?" [Looks around table.]

Leader: "You're saying that love in action can be justice. That is, we have said that a responsible leader has to take some action. It would be injustice not to act. So, if you really care about people for whom you are responsible, you'll make some decisions. So, the concern and the action do go together. Our question is about the action that will maximize the good of others and minimize the hurt to a long-term employee."

As the discussion continued, several key questions emerged, which we will present in this chapter:

- **How sure am I in my position in the company—and how confident am I in my own abilities as a decision maker?**
- **What are the demands made on me by top management, and by subordinates, that I must reasonably expect to meet?**
- **How can I balance concern for individuals and organizational goals in promotions to higher positions?**

- **Can I be fair and firm when I have to fire, transfer, or retrain someone?**

Do I Hold the Balances Steady?

Justice is founded on stable leadership. If you hold up the scales with a sure hand, you can weigh the needs of an individual and the group with more precision. And you will hurt another person less when you have to say that the scales are against him. Why? Because you are confident of your basic ability to make good decisions. You don't have to defend yourself or try to think up excuses. You can look openly at the problem with an individual who will need some help in realigning himself in the company and maybe in readjusting his self-concept.

If you are not sure of yourself as a decision maker, and uncertain of support from above and below, you may settle for sentimentality instead of justice, as we will see in the following case:

Mr. Kraft became branch manager at age 32. It was the first time that the bank in this suburb had such a young manager. He seemed very conscientious and was able to express his ideas in an attractive way. The women tellers thought that he was "darling." Mr. Kraft was an alert manager and soon noticed that the loan officer was not following the newer practices and policies of the bank. In fact, he openly criticized newer policies to his subordinates. One of them, Mr. Jamison, asked Mr. Kraft on several occasions if he knew what the loan officer was doing and saying. The manager said that he knew what was happening, and that he appreciated the concern of Mr. Jamison. He did not indicate that he would do anything. Later, Mr. Jamison told Mr. Kraft that he would resign if he continued to be criticized by the loan officer for making loans according to the instructions of the central office. Mr. Kraft said he was sorry to hear this and hoped that things could be worked out so that Mr. Jamison and his superior could work together in harmony.

Mr. Kraft then decided that as manager he should discuss the discrepancies in policy with the loan officer. When the men talked, the loan officer became angry and said that if the new manager wanted his job, he could have it. Mr. Kraft said that he did not mean to make him angry and that he was not casting any reflections upon his competence as a loan officer. After that conversation, the officer was openly belligerent towards the manager and more insistent that his subordinates follow the "sound practices" that he had been using for years. Tellers were aware of the tension and kept to themselves.

When Mr. Jamison resigned, his supervisory loan officer refused to give him a recommendation. Mr. Jamison was angry enough to ask the vice-president of personnel to intervene. When the vice-president talked to Mr. Kraft, the latter explained that he had hoped by good example to change the attitude of his loan officer. He wondered if Mr. Jamison was really competent since he had not been able to be patient with his superior officer.

The vice-president sat forward in his chair and said: "You mean to tell me that an employee who has been following our policies is not defended against that [expletive deleted]? If you know that an officer of your bank is trying to sabotage our new plan, put him on probation and then fire him if he continues to act that way. Meanwhile, write a strong recommendation for Jamison and start acting like a man."

Mr. Kraft was hurt and puzzled by this conversation. First, he was angry at the vice-president, then at himself. After several days of thinking, his anger against the loan officer finally came to the surface (after a customer had complained about the many delays in getting a loan application). Kraft sternly demanded that the officer make changes in his decision and speed up the loan process. He was amazed to find that the officer was quiet and efficient for several days. By this time, Kraft felt very uneasy. He had spoken harshly to a subordinate and could not look him in the eye. After several days of guilt, the manager apologized to the officer for getting angry. Later, the officer told his remaining subordinate: "Well, I told you I was right. He apologized for talking to me the way he did. Maybe he is beginning to see how things should really be run around here."

I have given this lengthy negative example because of the popular assumption that good interpersonal relationships in business are to be equated with compromise and sentimentality. This is a common delusion of inexperienced or inadequate executives. Since they are not really sure of themselves, they cannot be firm under threatening circumstances. They either fear that they will hurt themselves or that they will hurt someone else. Also, they may not be very sure about the organization and their place in it. This causes additional difficulties. *A strong decision depends both upon the adequacy of the individual and the security of his place in management.*

The opposite of sentimentality is the realistic exercise of love in a responsible organization. Love in action is justice. It is the judicious balance of the rights of an individual with the greatest good of a group. Since we live in organizations (family, church, club, company), we must consider both the rights of others and our own best interests. If we have a position of responsibility in an organization, then we are expected to exercise power on behalf of all the people in that organization. Unless we are willing to exercise that power in a responsible manner, we destroy justice. Someone must protect the basic rights of individuals in a group, and someone must make some discriminating judgments: who is going to be promoted, who is going to be put down? These are the realistic demands that can be met by an administrator who is sure of himself and the purposes of his organization.

What Demands Must I Meet?

What demands must you meet as a manager? There was a time when this could be answered on a quantitative basis by adding up production figures. You were responsible to stockholders for an adequate return on their investment. Employees were responsible to you for the efficient use of resources to produce goods that would sell at a profit.

Today you are responsible for product *and* people. If you do not value the persons with whom you work, then you are accused of injustice, inequality, discrimination.

If we are going to handle these new demands, we must develop some control over them. This begins by asking a classic question in ethics, what are you *obligated* to offer another human being? The assumption is that justice must be based upon what a person is due. A man must have some rights in order to be due something. That is, he must be owed something. So the question is, what do we owe him as an employee? What does top management or the board of directors owe to us? What do the employees owe us as managers?

It may seem strange to ask this kind of question when we already know what is required by federal safety and state hygiene regulations. Fair employment practices have detailed the rights of employees down to the number and length of coffee breaks and the exact requirements for overtime pay. The federal program against discrimination to minorities is massive and detailed. So what is there left for us to decide?

Employee expectations are often more subtle than safety or EOCC regulations. The concepts of what is due an employee are "hygiene" factors that Frederick Herzberg found in his study of Pittsburg industry.[1] The hygiene factors are preventative and environmental: the nature of the policies of the company and administrative practices under which a job is performed, the type of supervision that is received on the job, the quality of working conditions, the salary. These are the areas in which employees most commonly express dissatisfaction. They might be summarized in the study by Ross and Zander on dissatisfied employees as the "right to be recognized."[2]

The basic demand is for significance. It is not a "pure" request for recognition as an individual, but for recognition in relation to a specific task that is needed in this organization. The person wants to know that he and his job has a significant place in your mind. If the policies of the de-

---

[1] Frederick Herzberg, "New Approaches in Management Organization and Job Design," *Industrial Medicine and Surgery,* Vol. 31, 1962.

[2] See Indian Ross and Alvin Zander, "Need Satisfactions and Employee Turnover," *Personnel Psychology,* Vol. 10, 1957.

partment, the practice of supervisors, the conditions under which he works are those which do not cause him to feel valued, then you will be accused of injustice.

This accusation of injustice arises from conditions that may seem trivial. It is the common features of everyday life and work that cause people to see equality or inequality in their treatment.

There could be no more humble example than the "coffee-pot episode" in a hospital.[3] Management had agreed that good relations might grow out of staff conversations around a coffee-pot. But when doctors, nurses and aides discussed the making of coffee, there was resentment and dismay. The female attendants were resentful because they were asked to make the coffee. It was just one example of "women's work." The doctors were dismayed at the negative results of their good intentions. The nurses were insulted that the doctors had first requested them to take care of the coffee. The doctors resented a suggestion that everybody take turns. They were too busy for such tasks.

When people are resentful of slights or inconsiderateness in so many different areas, we have to agree on some priorities. What is due them above all else? An answer can be found in group discussions similar to those of doctors, nurses, and aides. It usually appears that people are not asking us to make them happy all over. They want to feel significant as workers when they are here at the plant. They do not hold us acceptable for their private satisfactions in life.

By asking "what is due?" we can bring into focus the

---

[3] Walter H. Bradshaw, Jr., "The Coffee-Pot Affair: An Episode in the Life of a Therapeutic Community," *Hospital and Community Psychiatry,* Vol. 23 #2, February, 1972.

primary demands for justice in a particular situation. The contract that we make with an individual employee is for our care of him in relation to this particular service. It is not like a marriage contract in which we obligate ourselves to total devotion. We really cannot take responsibility for some sources of employee dissatisfactions. For example, a study of the medical records of women employees of a company in Houston, Texas, showed that a small number of employees accounted for most of the sick days during any one year. These employees reported chronic social dissatisfaction. If they were single or divorced, they complained that they had to work for a living. If there were a parent at home, they complained of support for the parent.

In contrast, women employees with a few days of sick leave were not dissatisfied with their home conditions. If they were married, they were satisfied, and if they were divorced, they expressed relief. They were happy to be making their own way in life. If aged parents lived at home, they expressed satisfaction in what they were doing for the parents and the companionship of these loved ones.

It is true that a company may offer some personnel counseling for those who are dissatisfied with their home life, but no classic theory of justice would hold a manager responsible for a woman's satisfaction with her marriage or dissatisfaction with her divorce. In ethical theory, we are judged according to that for which we are accountable, as the provision of a living wage so that a person can care for aged parents, or equal pay to men and women, black and white.

Justice is the balance of concern for an individual and

a group. We recognize the outside influences that bear upon a person's job performance or satisfaction without allowing these problems to predominate over what is expected on the job. A senior executive told how he handled this problem with an employee who had become depressed. The employee, a bookkeeper, might stare out the window most of a day. The executive knew from social contacts of a family problem that weighed down this employee. Since the executive had a responsibility both to the company and to the employee, he said that the bookkeeper must immediately enter psychotherapy or be terminated. The company employee insurance plan provided the necessary funds for treatment. Although the bookkeeper first denied that he had any problems and promised to do better, the executive was firm. The bookkeeper then consulted the company psychologist, told him that it was of no use to talk, but he would have to do this or be fired. The psychologist replied that the man must be valued by his supervisor for the supervisor to insist that he receive help. During the first few interviews, the psychologist often reminded the despairing bookkeeper that he must be worth something to someone, or he would not have been sent for these interviews.

In this case, the recognition of a man on the job was the basis for his renewal of self-esteem. At the same time, the employer was not trying to meet *every* need of an employee. He did not offer personal counsel himself or try to make up for the affection that the man was not receiving in his own home.

This point is often made by the wives of executives. They believe that their husbands should notice members of their staff, especially when the staff members were going through some time of personal difficulty. But they consistently advise the husband to show interest without becoming involved. A wife reported with approval that her husband was always concerned when one of his secretaries looked depressed, and always had time for conversation with one who would explain why she was preoccupied on this particular day. If, as in one instance, the preoccupation came because of divorce proceedings, the executive recommended a marriage counselor and authorized several hours of leave each week for the secretary to see the counselor. "But," said the wife, "he didn't try to act as the counselor himself. He didn't have the time for it, and that was not his business."

Who Gets Promoted?

There are two questions about justice for any manager. One is the problem of basic rights for individuals, which we have just considered. This is called "compensatory" justice, the restoring of a balance, the provision of equality for each person.

We have heard so much about "equal rights," which is the function of compensatory justice, that we often forget the other type of justice, which is "distributive." This is the accuracy and fairness of our judgment in the exercise of power over people. It has to do with the distribution of rewards and penalties.

Distributive justice demands distinctions between persons to whom we are responsible. You will be making these kinds of judgments when you decide on the person who is to be promoted, the amount of bonus for a vice-president, the allocation of resources to departments.

The most troublesome of these decisions is reported to

be: "Who do I promote?" As one president of a company said: "You agonize over promotions. Will a man be helped or ruined? The man thinks that he wants to move from salary to commission. It looks good to him—the jump from $22,000 to $30,000 or $40,000. But can he really stand the pressure? Does he have the ability to move away from a secure position into one that depends entirely upon his initiative?"

This kind of decision is especially difficult when the employee will blame you for any failure that he experiences in the future. He will say that the general manager should never have allowed him to get into this position, or that he was not given enough support, or that he should have been told about some of the problems that he would face.

Why is it that you have more trouble with these kinds of judgments than you do with the allocation of resources in a plant or an agency? The usual answer is that a plant investment decision is based on research. Quantitative aids are provided for executives to make decisions with a minimum of risks.

When executives think about the promotion or transfer of people, they are changing a person's life. The hazards are greater if we are high in the management hierarchy and are voting on the advancement of a manager with ten or fifteen years of middle management experience. This is in contrast to the decision that we might make about a junior executive in his first year of management responsibility. If he fails, then he may be advised to change his field of interest or move to a different company. He has not lost as much as the district manager who seems to be failing as a new vice-president in the home office.

Several answers to the problem of senior promotions are mentioned in executive discussions. One is a feeling that every executive will take some risk if he competes with others for advancement. If he is not willing to accept the risks that go with a new position, then he should cross himself off of the eligible list and accept second place with grace, or take early retirement. A regional manager expressed his acceptance of this risk when he said: "My wife and I have really enjoyed life here in Atlanta. But if I do not accept the transfer to a higher position in Cleveland, they won't consider me but one more time for advancement. I still have ten good years, and I want to make the best of them." This man was in his late forties, his children were in college, and his wife was willing to move. His situation was quite different from that of another executive in the same company who had made the same move several years before. His children, in grade school and high school, were dislocated by the transfer, and his wife was so lonely that she killed herself within one year after the transfer.

There are risks that a man must accept in a move to another city, or in new responsibilities in the same location. When we discuss these risks with him, we are using a second suggestion that comes from executive seminars on ethics. This is to share with an eligible person the advantages and disadvantages of a move up the corporate ladder. What will it mean to him, his family and the company for this to happen?

The sharing of responsibility for the decision will be one way to distribute justice. In part, it is an open discussion with someone who may be promoted. Another part is our discussion with others who have some responsibility for a decision about this individual.

Are you willing to talk with others, including the one that may be promoted? If so, you are exhibiting a part of "temperance" that is important for justice. You are recognizing that no perfect decision can be made by an individual. All of your calculations are limited. You can take some of the responsibility for a man's future, but he will have to take some of this himself. There also are some unpredictable elements, or predictable ones that change for or against an individual.

A just decision requires accuracy and fairness, not omnipotence. You are judged ethically on your ability to weigh the factors for and against a promotion, discuss these realistically with all of the persons who would be affected by such a decision and the resoluteness with which you make a decision and support the person in whatever is decided.

Sometimes the decisions are very personal, as when we are dissolving a partnership with a brother or weighing the value of more money for a company officer who is our brother-in-law versus the declaration of a dividend to stockholders, which includes a widowed aunt who is solely dependent upon this revenue. This is such an involved issue that we will consider an actual case in more detail in chapter six.

The New Claims

There are some new claims from society that complicate criteria for promotions. The principal claim, presented with force by economic opportunity groups for the disadvantaged, is that offices and positions must be distributed with the greatest benefit to the least advantaged. John Rawls has elaborated this demand in *The Theory of Justice*. His answer to the current inequities of social and economic distribution is to place the rights of the disadvantaged above the economic advantages of a company. Managers have a "natural" duty to benefit the underprivileged, whether or not their decision will maximize future utilities. This is in keeping with Rawl's basic assumption that self-respect is the foundation of a just society. The most advantaged will gain self-respect by deploying their talents in the service of the least advantaged. This ethical criteria will become the basis for organizational decisions.[4]

Executives are depressed by the way in which this theory is implemented. One shook his head and said: "It just isn't fair for me to promote a black with two years of experience over a competent white person with ten years experience, just because we haven't met the EOCC quota of blacks in middle management." Other members of that discussion group agreed that more persons from minority groups should be advanced, but should it be at the expense of majority group members who had worked hard and faithfully for promotion? If there is only one position, who gets it?

A classic theory of distributive justice[5] would move toward an answer through three assumptions:

Assumption 1: A manager gives to each what his rank deserves. No exact calculation of

---
[4] John Rawls, *The Theory of Justice* (Cambridge: Belknap Press of the Harvard University Press, 1971), pp. 302, 102, 256.

[5] See Aristotle, *Nicomachean Ethics*.

rights is possible. Someone in authority must make a decision based on many factors, some more easily quantified than others. (In compensatory justice, we should be able to calculate the approximate amount of damage to a person's car in an accident and "compensate" him. But it is difficult to determine market value for decisions of distributive justice, which carry with them qualitative factors such as self-esteem, comparisons with others, etc.)

Assumption 2: Since more than actual market value is involved in distributive justice, some appeal must be made to society's standards for a good life. We must go beyond the internal criteria of profit and loss to consider the externalities of "the common good." Today, that is defined as special consideration for minority groups. A company is judged by its contribution to the common good by hiring a percentage of women, blacks, Indians, or Mexican-Americans as skilled laborers, managers, and executives. These are the externalities of personal justice, similar to the social justice demands for control of pollutants.

Assumption 3: Decisions of distribution rest more upon the prudence and justice of a manager than upon regulations from the state. The state has obligation to define the "common good" and enforce compliance in public and private sectors of the economy, but this is not maximized through the quantification of justice or the minute examination of employee records.

Executives are especially sensitive to this last assumption. They resent the attempts of government investigators to determine just who should be promoted or denied promotion. If the manager has a sense of justice and knows how to get things done (prudence), he will rapidly advance qualified persons from minority groups and encourage training programs to qualify more for job opportunity. He will also examine his criteria for advancement to see if they are racially or socially discriminatory.

But, the implementation of distributive justice must be with the executive. The very idea of "distribution" calls for an authority who makes distinctions. Society may set the criteria of "common good" that guides the manager in elevating one employee and bypassing another, but it cannot control the process of promotion in an organization. That is, unless society wishes to take over the organization by duplicating the executive function and monitoring all decisions. This calls for a vast expenditure of money, the training of public employees for judgments about complicated issues in the private sector, and a reduction of the initiative and responsibility of executives.

The last of these consequences is the most morally objectionable. The principal efforts of society should be toward the commitment of managers to "the common good" as a criteria of distributive justice. The executive function would be to bring this externality into the internal workings of the organization as we saw in the last chapter. A Southern manager used the social influence of nationwide publicity to change personnel policy in favor of blacks. Because he desired this, was in a position to know when it should be done, and was respected by the board of directors, the policy was effective. This is the circumstance under which distributive justice works best.

Our study has been aimed at this deepest level of value, the realm of interpersonal relationships where a man must know who he is and how he lives with others. The questions in the preceding chapters have been designed to lead toward a realistic analysis of what is truly important to us and how we can maximize our values throughout a company. We have been trying to find an answer to the question, how can I create a moral climate from the executive office?

But why should we be concerned to live this way? In previous chapters we have seen the answers of some executives. They believe that this is the best way to develop ingredients of enduring working relationships.

I am not arguing for "nothing but" individual initiative. Some "government interference" may be necessary in insensitive firms, and definitive policy from top management must shape the sentiments of reluctant managers. But the main direction must be the increase of a sense of justice and skill in its implementation by managers. An example of the combination of social, managerial, and individual movement toward distributive justice would be the seminars on equal opportunity for Detroit executives. Aaron Rutledge and other professional counselors who have worked with black employees met with managers of a plant to ask: "Now that you know that there will be three blacks in your management team by this time next year, what are some of your feelings about this change?" A day is spent in open confrontation of this issue by the men and women who really have the responsibility to see that promotions are profitable to both the individuals and the company.

Is This Firing Fair?

The distribution of privileges and penalties is always difficult when an "externality" is present. One of these is the common good, the demands of society for "affirmative action" toward those who are not of our class or color. Another externality is friendship with a colleague. How can we make a fair judgment when it must be against someone whom we enjoy socially? Or, most difficult of all, how can we dismiss a junior officer whom we have trained and trusted? We're cutting off a part of ourselves!

It's not *too* bad when the dismissal is an economic necessity. A manager may receive instruction to reduce the number of middle managers or to abolish particular positions as part of a reorganization to strengthen the competitive position of a company. Under these conditions, the executive can show his friend an order that answers the plaintive question: "Why me?"

The ethical obligation of an executive is to share information as quickly and completely as possible with all of the persons affected. This sounds reasonable, but many managers are loathe to go through the pain of such an interview, and therefore postpone the news that is really necessary for a person to make plans for his future. This lack of courage is an injustice.

When a decision must be made, executives may try to make up "externalities." We may insinuate that someone with influence in the company is prejudiced against the person when we really are dismissing him because of incompetence. But by cunning we divert disappointment from us to some nebulous "they." The result is a suspicion cast upon some powerful group, such as a board of directors, who trust us and count on us to support policy. All that we gain is temporary ease of circumstances with a friend who has to go.

How will you feel tomorrow about the man that you fired today? Right now your answer might be: "Worried. I have spents nights thinking what will happen to his wife and family. I wonder what prospective employers think when I cannot write a strong recommendation."

But if you are forthright in a discussion of the problems with a person at the earliest opportunity, you will probably find that both of you feel better tomorrow. For example, a vice-president found that one of his managers was falsifying financial records. At first the vice-president could not believe this because he had trained the manager and had been his friend for ten years. The vice-president asked his wife how such a problem could arise with people whom they trusted and enjoyed. The wife shared his concern, even when he would toss and turn at night without sleep, trying to decide what to do. They finally decided that one of the big problems was the breach of trust. The vice-president would have to admit his disappointment in the younger man before he could talk objectively to him about dishonesty.

When the vice-president could admit to himself that this bothered him more than his concern for the man's family or future, he was ready to talk with the manager. It was a straightforward conversation in which the vice-president told him what he had learned and how he had learned it. The manager gave a great sigh of relief and said that he had been dreading this moment for almost a year. He had been going into debt for three years to place his children in fashionable schools and impress associates in an expensive club. For the last year he had used company funds to pay some of these expenses.

> **Vice-president:** "I had no idea that you were that far beyond your means. I know that you love your family, but I did not know that it would come to this."
> **Manager:** "Well, they did not know. I tried to keep up appearances with them. Of course my wife knew that something was wrong because I became a heavy drinker on the weekends. I could not stand to live such a lie, and I knew that they would be hurt by the truth [voice breaks]. She is so trusting. She thought that I was drinking because of pressures at work or new associates in the club. She kept asking what she could do to help. Well, nothing could help except a conversation like this."
> **Vice-president:** "Oh, now I know what you mean about being relieved to talk. I was puzzled about that."
> **Manager:** "You have always been my friend. You have always been straight with me. I guess you had to be this way with me for me to be

this way with you—but it certainly took me a long time. I should have talked to you a year ago. [Pause] But at least we have talked now. I don't have to lie any more, and I don't have to drink any more."

Vice-president: "OK, Charlie. Now how about the people we have to talk with? You need to talk with Sarah [wife], and I need to talk with the president about the reason for your dismissal. There will be some legal action. Can you take that OK without getting back to the drink?"

Manager: "Sure, sure. It will be rough, but you cannot imagine how much better I feel already. And I will feel much better after Sarah and I have talked. I'll tell the auditors everything."

Subsequent events showed that the manager could stay sober when he had made a clean confession. He continued to appreciate the vice-president. For his part, the vice-president began to realize that he had not hurt his friend unnecessarily because he had first faced the hurt that had been done to him. Once he had recognized his own disappointment in someone whom he had trusted, he did not try to make the man feel guilty for that which he could not change, a breach of trust. What he could change was his behavior, and the open conversation assisted the manager to be honest about what he had done.

What about the social relationships? At first, Sarah felt that she could never go shopping with the vice-president's wife again or be a guest in their home. She was surprised to find that her older friend was not only willing to see her but supportive of Charlie's decision to tell the truth. She told Sarah that now a barrier had been removed to a better relationship between husband and wife and that her husband was especially pleased to know that Charlie's secret drinking had stopped.

This is an illustration of the quality of mercy in justice. Without a forgiving and trusting spirit, the administration of justice can become cruelty.

The quality of mercy is shown in the way that we administer justice. Do we keep our own feelings at a minimum and think of the person who is being disciplined and the other persons who are affected in the organization? Many times the appellation of "justice" or the accusation of "injustice" about one of our decisions is more a question of the way in which we exercise discipline than the basic decision to transfer, demote, or fire an employee. We are judged both by the substance of our decisions and the manner in which they are made.

4

When And How Do I Act?

The new president of a retail company was faced with an ethical dilemma when the manager of his largest store told him: "Inventory is a mess. There are continual complaints that we do not stock items that are advertised, and yet we consistently overstock dry goods that have to be dumped in a 'white sale' every six months. That department chief doesn't coordinate anything, but he knows everybody. Now that you are going to reorganize, what will you do about inventory?"

The manager went on to say that he had discussed this problem on many occasions with Mr. Jameson (who was in charge of inventory) and was always told that things would be corrected, or that everything was in good order. The manager felt that Mr. Jameson did not know what was really going on in each department and was not interested in making any changes. Yet he was an employee with many years of service who had always managed to be on good terms with the president of the company and several members of the board of directors.

The president decided that Mr. Jameson should not be told again of his deficiencies. This would only result in an argument. Instead, the president would tell Mr. Jameson that a part of his reorganization included inventory reports to the president's office from each store in a region. Responsibility for inventory control in each store would be with the resident manager. Mr. Jameson could have his choice of working as a buyer in one of several departments and retain his present salary.

When the manager told Mr. Jameson of an appointment that he would have with the new president, Jameson asked the reason for this meeting and the manager told him that it was connected with the questions that the manager had been raising about inventory control over the past few years. "Oh" said Jameson, "then you really have not been satisfied with the work that I have been doing." The manager said that this was a part of the problem and that he had discussed it with the president. However, it would be up to the president to say what his new organizational scheme would be for the central office and how inventory would fit into this.

The president said nothing about his dissatisfaction with the work of Mr. Jameson in their private interview. Instead, he attempted to sell Jameson on the value of a centralized system of inventory control. Mr. Jameson said that he would step down as necessary from any position that he had and would accept whatever the store manager offered him. Immediately upon his return to the store, Mr. Jameson told many associates: "I wish that I had joined the union. There ought to be some way for a person at my level to state his grievances. I have just been done in by the new boss. He won't tell me that anything is wrong with my work, but I know that he has something against me. Now I am being fired without cause."

In the deluge of distrust that followed these accusations, the manager realized that he had done the right thing in the wrong way. He knew from conversations with many department chiefs that the new organization was acceptable and that Mr. Jameson could not control inventory. The basic decision was realistic. But he had allowed poor performance and reorganization to become so mixed that both reorganization and performance ratings were in jeopardy. He should have discussed this part of reorganization in more detail with his department chiefs. This would have secured their support, or at least maintained their trust when a change took place. He also should have been the one to tell Mr. Jameson that he did not fit into the new requirements of inventory control. He had allowed a superior to take some of his responsibility. (At the same time, he was grateful that directors of the board were calling the president rather than him for explanations of Mr. Jameson's transfer.)

The sadder and wiser manager has been confronted with the problems of prudent judgment: How do I make a realistic decision at the right time with good consequences? To fulfill these requirements, the manager would have needed an objective perception of what was actually going on between himself, the president, Mr. Jameson, and department managers. He would also have needed foresight, an ability to predict the way in which a specific action would lead toward the realization of a desirable goal.

Prudence is the most difficult virtue to exercise because it is based upon so many intangibles in our own decision and so many circumstances that change beyond our control or knowledge. Each situation is quite different from any other in specific outcome, although we can develop some basic guidelines that would see us through most decisions with a minimum of personal difficulty.

What we are looking for is more discriminating decisions. As Perrin Stryker stated in *The Character of the Executive,* "Increasing discrimination still seems to come closest to explaining, in one word, performances of the most competent executives and managers I have had the opportunity to observe." [1]

Classical ethics places prudence before all of the other virtues because it is the one that deals with the application of that which is good to that which is realistic in the world. Unless a decision is based upon reality, it cannot be true. No matter how "good" our intentions, an unrealistic decision is immoral. An ethical choice must be true (realistic) before it can be good (ideal).

A word of caution is necessary. We are so accustomed to being pragmatic that we think this is "prudent." That is, we make so many decisions to avoid embarrassing situations or to be a clever tactician that we escape personal commitment. This kind of cunning and cowardice is condemned in classical ethics. A man is expected to be brave, honest, and so committed to standards of justice that he will risk temporary inconvenience or permanent disfavor for the sake of what he personally believes to be right. But the risk must be based on a realistic appraisal of what is actually going on. A foolish or stupid decision cannot be excused by reference to some ethereal ideal. The ideals must be high, but they must be applied with accuracy.

---

[1] Perrin Stryker, *The Character of the Executive,* p. 26.

From a moral point of view, an executive is required to have bifocal vision. He must have a strong view of what *ought* to be, but it must be guided by what *is* right now. Prudence is practical without sinking to the manipulation and compromises of pragmatism. The ethical imperative is to do that which is good, but that is only possible when you know what is going on in yourself and others.

Am I Honest With Myself?

In commenting on a case of inflated progress reports, Paul A. Teegarden, president and indirect owner of Columbus Asphalt Corporation, said that he faced the same problem when he was an accounting manager. He laid the facts on the line to his boss who did nothing. When Teegarden took the problem to a higher authority and was stopped, he quit. At that time, he insisted on handing in reports that contained the bad news and expected management to listen to him or lose money.

Later, when he had his own business, he made the same mistake. He allowed his enthusiasm to keep out the bad news even though he had previously vowed that he would never let it happen. There was no specific way for people to disagree with his view of production. He fired a manager who dissented. When he realized what he was doing, he developed a system of reporting to the manager which must always include a positive statement that all dissenting views are included.[2]

Mr. Teegarden illustrated the first question of prudence, "Am I honest with myself?" It is the question that we have already faced in our discussion on temperance. Do we know

---

[2] John J. Sendrock, "Sequel to Quasar Stellar," *Harvard Business Review,* Sept.-Oct., 1968, p. 18.

ourselves well enough to keep our own feelings from getting in the way of a correct estimate of a situation? Since we have already discussed the importance of self-knowledge, we must move to talk about the way in which we structure relationships so that honesty will be maximized and self-deceit minimized.

The usual recommendation is for a check on the accuracy of information through a variety of authoritative persons who are close to the senior manager. But this system will not work unless the senior partner is able to look *with* his associates at a problem. If he thinks that they are directly criticizing him by disagreements or the presentation of alternatives, any system of participant management will soon be abandoned.

So, you have to ask yourself the question: "Just how big do I think I am?" If you think that you must know everything and have all of the answers, you will be making many decisions based on unreality. This will happen in part because of your own distortion of what you hear and in part upon the unwillingness of subordinates to tell you the full picture or to test your interpretations against their perception of reality.

I believe that this ability to be honest with yourself is a character trait that is well formed in childhood and does not change much into adult life. My impression was confirmed by some remarks of Junior Chamber of Commerce executives who said that the ability to accept criticism is something that goes back to childhood. As I would see it, someone must have cared for us enough for us to be basically secure about our place in the world. At the same time, important people must have frustrated some of our desires to do exactly what we wanted to do or to see things just our own way. If we got more acceptance than frustration, we grew up with an increasingly realistic view of ourselves and others. We would know that the occasional criticisms of some of our views or manners were not going to devastate us.

One junior executive put it this way: "So what if my boss makes a crack about the way that I walk, or some secretary says that my shoes look awful? I don't go off in a corner and cry about that. I just think about what is worth changing. Maybe I could stand a little straighter, but I don't think that I can change the way that I walk. The shoes —well, maybe I should not wear those crepe soled loafers so much. And I guess I should not put my feet on my desk. Anyway, why get all shook up about things like that? If you are smart, you will change the things that *really* count."

It takes a strong ego to say that. In contrast, a "big" ego would be deflated. Why? Because the inadequate person tries to protect himself by acting as though he is above criticism. One pinprick will take all the air out of his balloon.

It takes a certain amount of personal character to accept criticism. Character is strengthened by the rewards that we receive in business. People accept us if we admit our mistakes and demonstrate an awareness of how we can do better. When we accept responsibility for our share of a difficulty, subordinates feel that we are honest about our humanity and superiors believe that we can be trusted. We show that we are placing the good of the company above the protection of our own self-image. Obviously, it is not long before we also realize that this kind of honesty is good for us as well. It is not only a basic part of our character, it is also the ingredient of integrity that commends us to higher responsibility.

However, as a number of executives stated in their review of the "Quasar Stellar" (a case of inflated progress reports), there are some companies in which top management doesn't want to hear any bad news and resents criticism. Under those circumstances, a man may decide like Mr. Teegarden to quit the company, or he may keep quiet and hope that too many mistakes are not made before it is time for him to retire.

Am I Frank with Others?

The higher our responsibility, the more necessary is "unvarnished" honesty. Anything that we know about a particular issue must be revealed. If not, we are faced with the unhappy circumstances that Mr. Pierre duPont wrote about the resignation of Mr. Durant from General Motors. Mr. duPont had been open with other members of the board of directors about his stock in General Motors and Chevrolet, which were unpledged. He was not a buyer or seller of stock in any amount, and he certainly was not a borrower of money on his stock in the company, When Mr. Durant was asked if he knew of any weak accounts in the market, he said, no, and left the impression upon other directors that his holdings were as clear as theirs.

At a later meeting, Mr. Durant told the directors that "the bankers" had demanded his resignation as president of General Motors and that he acceded because he "was in the hands of the bankers." The next day Mr. duPont learned from Mr. Durant that he personally owed 14 million dollars to banks and brokers, against which he held three million shares of General Motors stock. He had no personal books or accounts and was unable to give definite statements as to the total indebtedness. He could not tell what part of a 20-million-dollar indebtedness was personal and what part was the indebtedness of others on which he had lent collateral without other commitment.[3]

Most professional managers in the last half of the twentieth century will not have the large personal financial investment in a company that was characteristic of executives in the 1920s. But the need for full disclosure of all details relating to a particular transaction is still valid. Executives in a seminar on ethics were unanimous in stating that a man who "shaded" the truth or did not tell the full story would not be trusted and soon would be moved out of the executive suite. The owner of a construction company said: "If a man does not give me the full story one time, I assume that he may have missed a few details, and I just warn him. But if he does this two or three times, and always seems to leave out the part that would make him look bad, I have to let him go or transfer him to some position where his information doesn't make any difference. Things are too complicated, and the market is too competitive for me to make a decision based upon imperfect or biased information. Of course, I never expect to hear everything that is going on or exactly what is going on, but I do expect to hear enough of the facts to make a good decision."

The remark of this executive combines trust and tolerance. On the one hand, he expects people to tell him as much as they know about details of a particular transaction. On the other hand, he does not expect them to be any more accurate in remembering details or in presenting

---

[3] Alfred P. Sloan, *My Years With General Motors,* pp. 32-35.

information than he is himself. The reason for a sharing of information and ideas is the minor imperfections and distortions among the individuals who are pondering a problem. We are all going to be human with limitations, but we can try to be honest.

It seems that executives "try harder" with those for whom they have specific responsibility. Managers say that they would be much less specific in describing the strengths and weaknesses of a person who was seeking a position in the company than they would be with someone whom they had supervised for months or years. They give several reasons for this. First, an applicant is not yet the responsibility of the manager. Therefore, it would not be appropriate for the manager to describe all the reasons for acceptance or rejection of a person with whom he has no specific relationship. Second, information for hiring a person may come from outside sources which the supervisor cannot evaluate. He is therefore more cautious in stating his opinion to this applicant. On the other hand, he would feel more obligation to say exactly what he thought to one of his subordinates whom he had observed at first hand and on whom he had evaluations from other trusted sources. Third, the supervisor would try to protect the company from any bad feelings or subsequent legal actions that might come from a prospective employee who is angered or insulted by specific personal evaluations. Since the applicant has no relationship to the company, he might conclude that it is filled with racial or other biases.

The degree of frankness is dependent upon the strength of a relationship. A manager is more apt to "tell the whole truth" to a person for whom he has some definite obligations. This obligation often combines responsibility for the individual and for the morale of an office. For example a young married man began to spend every coffee break with an attractive unmarried secretary. Soon the young man was going to lunch as well as to coffee with the secretary. When his supervisor warned him that he was using bad judgment, the young man stopped his visiting of the secretary for a few weeks, but then was back into the same habit. The supervisor told him again that there was much talk among employees of this relationship and that it would be recorded as an example of poor judgment when he was considered for advancement. Soon after this warning, the young man became drunk at the annual office party and had to be carried home. The next day, his supervisor said that this was further evidence of his lack of judgment and was cause for his dismissal.

It may seem from this distinction between frankness with employees and caution with applicants that executives are willing to be deceptive or dishonest. When I raised this question, executives said, "No!" As the managers see it, you have to be open about anything for which you have responsibility in the company.

The first reason given for consistent honesty is realism. An experienced executive knows enough about a company to realize that the truth about any transaction will eventually become known. A bank vice-president said that if he were to bribe a banking commission, some member of the commission would eventually tell someone in his bank. **Second, his executive must have a reputation for integrity for good people to be attracted to his employ.** If he is rumored to be deceitful, or known to be dishonest, more and more immoral or amoral subordinates will be attracted to his office, and soon the honest members of his department will give up and ask for a transfer. Since executives believe that their success depends upon the talents and character of those who work with them, a reputation for deceit is the same as personal disaster.

Third, the executives believe that honesty becomes more decisive as they move up in the company. Both employee and public respect are involved. They believe that staff members read the attitudes of top executives and act in accord with what they think will bring maximum approval. This was applied both to public administration, as in the Watergate case, and in the business world, as in the ITT case.

Fourth, the executives believe that a man who only told part of the truth, or who fabricated answers, would soon lose his ability to judge realistically. He would think that he could trick anyone. This is a deception. Also, he would spend so much time thinking about the cover-up that he would have little energy for objective reflection on what is actually happening around him. Furthermore, he would soon lose any associates who would be honest with him. He would be left with persons who thought like he did, and soon his own reason would be confused by the multiplicity of devious thoughts.

Fifth, so much energy would be spent on cover-ups that much less would be accomplished and stockholders would soon wonder about the lack of production and the splintering of morale. A comptroller gave the example of a builder who spent three-fourths of his energy on schemes that would prevent the payment of taxes to the government. The comptroller, who was naturally good at computations, had calculated the losses from this misuse of talent. For every thousand dollars that was saved through devious schemes against the government, the builder probably lost ten thousand dollars in sales from projects on which he should have spent his time.

The comptroller's estimate of the builder is an example of another question that comes up when we discuss honesty. How do others know that an executive is going to tell them the truth? One of the most telling clues is the activity of an executive off the job. This is so important that many companies invite a prospective manager and his wife to visit on a weekend at a club or resort away from the business. This is an opportunity to see the man and his wife under social conditions that do not relate directly to the work that he will do. What is his style of life? How directly does he relate to people? How do husband and wife relate to each other?

The basic assumption is that a man of integrity is going to tell the truth in *all* of his relationships. During an executive seminar in a major city, the president of a company observed that his roommate was out every evening with a different woman. Yet the roommate had unpacked a picture of his wife and children and placed it prominently on the dresser. The executive was thankful that his roommate did not bring the women into the room, but he did decide to avoid any business contact with the man in the future. As he reasoned, a man who would cheat on his wife would certainly cheat another company.

All-round integrity is secured in our mind when a person is willing to tell the truth even when it hurts. This is a sign that a manager places the good of the company above his personal convenience. The question for the executive is "Who will be hurt by what I tell?" If he is the one who will be embarrassed, then a full declaration brings him much credit. If his disclosure is to the public and causes injury to his company, it is difficult to know how to judge him. For example, an analyst for Equity Funding first advised his clients of financial difficulties and then told the Exchange about company problems. The Exchange reprimanded him for giving preferred treatment to his clients, but a number of executives told me that the analyst was correct in first advising those to whom he had direct responsibility. He did not conceal what he knew from the Exchange, but he did speak first to those who had retained his counsel.

Since the question of "telling the truth" to the public is often a matter of forecasting earnings for a company, some corporations opt for open disclosure. One bank gives three projections of earnings for a coming year, each one of which is based on different estimates of economic circumstances. Investors may then make their own decisions about the financial health of the institution.

In a staff meeting, executives would expect every person to speak his mind. Forecasting must be based upon corporate reasoning. The executives believe that this is more common today than thirty years ago because younger executives are not as security conscious. They are willing to risk more. They did not grow up in the scarcity of a depression. Also, general managers realize that modern companies are too complex for any one person to know exactly what to do. The facts must be presented by a variety of informed persons and then weighed by all those who have responsibility for a realistic forecasting and for analysis of past mistakes.

Why Do I Take This Action?

Values are very prominent when you have run out of facts and still have to project the program for the future. What are the general goals of the company to which this specific program must be related? The projection of programs and goals will demand both the prerequisites of prudence: (1) an objective projection of reality, (2) foresight on the impact of a particular action upon the realization of stated goals.

The capacity to hear varying opinions with respect is based upon something in our character that the psychologist Milton Rokeach has called "openmindedness." Dr. Rokeach has examined ways in which we incorporate new ideas and form opinions. He has found evidence that people are able to make genuine changes in their attitudes when they have believed from childhood that the world is a good place in which to live. Since these people feel secure in their surroundings, they do not need to be on guard against any new idea. They are not easily threatened.

In contrast, a person who has reason to believe from his early years that the world is a hostile place must always be on guard against the unexpected. These are "closed-minded persons" who vigorously reject any opinion that is not in line with the authority system that gives them security. They hold dogmatically to opinions expressed by some revered figure or party. Other persons are accepted or rejected according to the agreement or disagreement with this ultimate authority.

The opinions of a closed-minded person are not changed by facts or logic. His change of mind comes when we can cite evidence from his authority to support our reasoning.

Then he makes the change, not because of our reasoning, but because of his loyalty to an authority.[4]

A manager's ability to alter his opinions on the basis of other people's evidence will be based upon his world view. The man who believes that God's creation is good and that he can live in harmony with others, will listen attentively and make rational decisions. The man who believes that the world is full of evil and that no one is to be trusted, will listen only to a proven authority in his small security system. To him, there is only one answer to the question "Why do I take this action?" It must be a completely good decision based upon the principles of his authority, or it is an evil decision which he will continue to question as a "matter of principle."

Managers often criticize the dogmatic individual because he will not play on the team. He is a Monday morning quarterback who continues to criticize management decisions with which he was not in total agreement. But the closed-minded person does not think that he is disloyal. Actually, he believes that he is the only one who knows what is right and is trying to save the company from ruin. You cannot answer these persons. The best you can hope for is to isolate them in a position where they are not required to make many decisions. Give them strict rules from an authoritative source and they will persevere. They are quite dependable so long as they are not asked to change their minds.

You probably will not have gone very far in your company if you are dogmatic, but you may find some of the symptoms of dogmatism in occasional rigidity of your own

[4] The evidence for these opinions is presented by Milton Rokeach in *The Open and Closed Mind.*

thinking. At such a time you will have to confess that there was some threat to your system of values that caused you to reject the opinions of others and to say "this is it" no matter what others may say. Why would you take this particular course of action? Sometimes the threat may be to some basic value for which you should fight. The members of one executive seminar said that any executive should protest vigorously if an immoral decision is being made by the management team. As an illustration they condemned Fred La-Rue who testified that he remained in the "Watergate mess" because he did not think that he was a person with power to question those above him.

On other occasions we may find that we cannot listen because our personal security is too threatened. It is not a matter of what is good for the company or for society, but just a matter of our own income, status, or influence. Since this happens on occasion to anyone, the prudent executive is one who recognizes what is happening to him at the time, or immediately thereafter.

I still remember the stupid feeling I had after a meeting of hospital administrators. The administrators had just approved the formation of an accrediting association for chaplains. They had also debated the fee to be charged chaplains who wished to be examined for accreditation in the hospital organization. I argued against the proposal with reasons that caused several administrators to look at me with annoyance. I was so persistent that the proponents finally shrugged their shoulders and said that the question could be considered at a later time. That day we voted for the accrediting organization, without references to fees. By the next day I was relaxed enough to realize that I did not want an organization for clergymen to become as status conscious as other professional organizations in the health field. But what did the charging of fees have to do with my concern? I was determined to keep my mouth shut in the next day's business meeting, which considered and passed a modest examination fee for eligible chaplains. Well, who knows how rigid one will be when his profession, his pet project, his performance seems to be under attack? If we can think beyond the threat of the moment to the objective for a particular program, we may develop both insight and foresight.

Should I Act Now?

Since our insight is often skewed by personal interest and our foresight blurred by insufficient information, we may see the wisdom of Chester Barnard when he declared: "The fine art of executive decision consists in not deciding questions that are not now pertinent, in not deciding prematurely, in not making decisions that cannot be made effective, and in not making decisions that others should make." [5]

With all of these negatives, it would sound as though we would never act. But the warning of Professor Barnard is against those who try to assume too much responsibility, with little attention to the informal communication system of the organization, and to those who lack the ability to inhibit and modify their immediate desires. [6]

How will we know that an action is appropriate? The answer to this question will depend upon individual circumstances, but there are two prerequisites of character that must be considered.

---

[5] *Functions of the Executive,* p. 194.

[6] *ibid.,* pp. 225, 261.

First, a prudent executive has a sense of moral imperative. He knows that he must take the ultimate responsibility for decisions. Some action must be taken. If he lags behind others and consistently pleads for more information or discussion, he is probably trying to avoid possible threat to his own security. This raises the question of bravery, which we will consider in the next chapter.

The other characteristic is tolerance for uncertainty. A senior executive must absorb huge amounts of ambiguity. If you are in this position, you know that some of your trusted associates do not know any more than you do, and some of them are not going to tell you all that they do know. Even those who try will present the case with some bias. Then there are those agonizing times when two excellent solutions are presented by intelligent groups who have the good of the company at heart. How are you going to decide between them?

You can always ask yourself some standard questions, such as "What has happened beforehand to bring things to pass as they are right now?" and "What is the specific goal that we hope to realize through this particular action?" You also can be sure that the inner coalition of the management group is composed of representatives from all groups in the organization that are affected by major decisions. Still, you have to manage this coalition in such a way that the major goals of the organization are served despite inadequate information and conflicting alternatives.

In *Organizations in Action,* James Thompson recommends an open recognition of the uncertainties that subordinates present to senior managers. When you can talk openly about the unknown, group cohesion is increased and any decision will be better than a dogmatic or impulsive one. Professor Thompson notes that the flow of communication may be limited by managers who emphasize their office more than their function as mediators. The communication may also be subverted by family ties, patronage, bribery, or tradition.

If we can face these obstacles openly, we are in a better position to act realistically. A part of realism is the humble admission that we are not quite sure of ourselves and face some threat in whatever decision is to be made. When we have admitted this, we have taken the first step toward courage, which is to acknowledge fear. We can make more secure decisions for the future when we acknowledge the contingencies that shake us. This means that prudent decisions can only be carried out by brave men, who overcome their fear by rational planning for the future.

5

What Are The Consequences?

Executives test a moral decision by the question: "Will it last?" It is especially decisive in a day of short supply and swift changes of markets. An executive is consistently tempted to change his mind because his company will be advantaged by black market purchases or preferential treatment. He may be told that additional supplies of a scarce item such as gasoline are available in this quarter of the year. The distributor offers him gasoline today with the understanding that a record of the purchase will not be entered until the next quarter. It is difficult to think about tomorrow, to know that we must live with the memory of what we have done today.

Would an executive keep his word about a decision even when a change of circumstances will mean a financial loss for his company? A company promised steel to a contractor at one price, and then the price went up. The contractor felt that the integrity of the steel company was strengthened because they made delivery at the original price. The contractor recognized the dilemma of the company and tried to help by requesting some change in the specifications that the highway department had made in the amount of steel to be used in bridges. If the highway department would accept less steel without this causing a reduction of safety standards, then the contractor would feel that he had reduced the loss of profit to the steel mill.

In the long run, the integrity of an executive is judged more by his consistency despite pressures than by any other single criteria. This is the way that executives judge themselves. They ask: "Can I live tomorrow with the decision that I have made today?"

This is also a key issue in the confidence of junior executives in their senior managers. Junior Chamber of Commerce men say that they cannot tolerate a senior executive who says yes today but does not back you up tomorrow. Strength of character means keeping your word, standing by a difficult decision.

How do we develop and maintain this essential virtue, which is called fortitude?

Did I Count the Cost?

Fortitude begins in foresight. If we have thought out the consequences of a decision, we are more likely to face them with equanimity. This is true in all areas of life. One study of surgical patients showed that there was less distress and anxiety among patients who had been told what to expect before an operation. If they experience pain several days after the operation, they remember what the doctor told them to expect and how they should react. They were able to bear the discomfort because they had counted the cost before the surgery. In contrast, patients who were not briefed before surgery were the ones who complained the most and suffered the most anxiety and pain after an operation. They did not know what to expect, and they were angered or fearful of what they experienced.

Do you accept the possibility of pain after some important decision? IF you admit the ways in which you can be hurt by what you have done, you will be less open to disappointment with others and less likely to attack those who do not appreciate your efforts.

Disappointment usually arises from a naïve belief that what we have done is going to be understood and accepted by others. When the decision is misunderstood and we are criticized, our first impulse may be to reverse the decision. But then how consistent are we? Who will rely on a manager who acts so impulsively when he isn't appreciated?

The best antidote for disappointment is selflessness. In an earlier chapter we discussed this as a consistent balance between that which is good for others and that which is good for us. When we find that our greatest satisfaction comes in building up the program from which others benefit with us, we are less likely to look for some specific appreciation for our efforts. We believe that many persons will benefit in the long run from our judgment, and we are willing to accept some differences of opinion from those who may not understand the immediate results of our actions.

Of course, there are sometimes when we are really crushed by the response of those around us. Under these conditions, we might as well be human and admit our disappointment. If this is an occasional feeling and not a chronic search for approval, it will probably result in more support from the staff and a better understanding on the part of all parties.

When we let them know that their reaction really matters, they can see that we intended the best in what we did. With clarification today, we are better prepared for similar decisions tomorrow. We will not only be more complete in our knowledge of what is to be expected, staff members will also aid in the interpretation of our decisions by saying: "I am sure this is what he means by this memo."

But what if we are severely attacked and it really hurts? What prevents us from jumping on our persecutors? When the attack is unexpected, recognize your anger. Don't pretend that you are breathing hard because you walked up a flight of stairs or that your voice is trembling because you are getting older. If you know the signs of anger in yourself, you will have more control over the feeling as it is expressed.

Express what you feel to someone. For example, the director and five associates in an advertising department planned the promotion of a new product and went as two-man teams to potential buyers. Afterwards, each team planned to critique its presentation as well as the general structure of the advertising campaign.

After several weeks of promotion, the director found himself with an artist who had previously worked directly with the assistant director of the department. The director had always thought the artist to be a pleasant fellow who was responsible in his work. He was surprised when the artist was habitually late for appointments with clients and even more surprised at what happened when they talked about this:

Director: "You certainly make up for lost time

when you finally get to the meeting and begin your presentations. It is excellent. But I think that we are losing ground with some of these people, and we certainly are losing time. They have other things to do with their time, and so do I. Be on time for the rest of our appointments."

Artist: [Expletive deleted.] "Get off my back about my schedule! You set those meetings at a lousy time. I need coffee and a good breakfast before I can get started. Then you whiz around so fast all day that nobody can ever catch up."

Director: "If you can't keep up the pace, go back to your drawing board. I can carry the rest of these assignments myself."

Artist: "Do you want to know what I think of the way you carry these assignments? [Director nods.] I say you have not done [expletive deleted]. I would have thought that a man in your position and with your training would have really carried the ball in these conversations. But you drop it, and I have to pick it up."

Director: "Are you just giving your own opinion, or did you hear something from some of the clients?"

Artist: "Well, I heard one of them say after yesterday's presentation that you rambled a good deal."

Director: "Anything else?"

Artist: "Well, isn't that enough? I have always respected you and thought that you had a great deal to offer. If you don't think I have anything to offer on this trip, tell me so, and I'll get back to my other work."

Director: "I'll be talking to Carl [the assistant director] in a little while, and then we'll make a decision."

The artist went off to the bar, and the director was left alone in the hotel room, waiting for his long distance call. He regretted the economy measure of two men in one room. He was thoroughly disgusted with his impulsive associate and wondered if he should have fired him on the spot. Then the phone rang.

It was Carl. After a few moments of discussion about the associate director's activities, the director said:

Director: "Look, this little [characterization deleted] just bit me on the ankle. He may be an artist to you, but he is a pain in the neck to me. He's all buddy-buddy until you cross him, and then he spits on you."

Carl: "Yeah, I know. He does that to me, but I put him to work by himself and just check on his assignments periodically. I get him to agree on what he is going to do, and then he has to judge himself. He can't control his temper at first, but then he settles down."

Director: "Well, I am not settled down! I didn't let him have it because you've been respon- sible for his work ever since he came into our department. So I wanted to check with you before I said anything to him."

Carl: "So what did you want to tell him?"

Director: "Well, I first thought of firing him. I still may do that. That's why I wanted to talk to you."

Carl: "Well, I'm glad that you did. That's your right, and you have cause. But there are two problems. He is a good layout man, and he really turns out the work. But most important, if you fire him when it's just the two of you, he will come back here and say that *you* lost your temper when he told you how bad your work was. What will that do to our idea of sharing criticism without anybody feeling that they are going to get the axe because of it?"

Director: "That's right, that's right. He would really make me look bad. Well, more important, he would make our idea of 'peer review' look bad."

Carl: "Are you really interested in keeping up with that peer review? Some of us have wondered if you wanted to stick with it."

Director: "Do you think I would have spent all that money on the management consultant if I was not serious? Sure, and I intend to take it as much as anybody else. Every man should listen to criticism and learn for his own good and for the sake of our program. It's a new one, and we've got to try it out together."

Carl: "So what could you tell Oren [the artist] along that line?"

Director: "Well, I could tell him that the success of our new way of doing things will depend on every man keeping his temper and—well, I could tell him if he insults me, he will probably insult other people on our teams as well. So he will just discourage everybody from saying what they think, because he attacks before he thinks."

Carl: "That's right, you are telling him something that is for the good of the whole department, and not just a personal reaction that he could twist into vindictiveness because your pride was hurt. Of course, you are angry, I can tell."

Director: "You're [expletive deleted] right! But it will be about the program and the way he has got to stop this with everybody, including me—and you."

Carl: "OK. If he can take it, let him stay with you, if you can stand him in the same room. He's a very charming fellow when he wants to be."

Director: "Sure, sure, as long as we don't cross him, he's just fine. Well, that day is over, and I will keep my temper until I see you again to talk about any further action on this. Meantime, I have got the speech prepared. Thanks."

The director had talked to the right person. He learned from talking with Carl how costly it would be to express his own anger in a way that Oren could use against him with the whole department. The new program of open critique would have been jeopardized. The director was glad that he had not retaliated when Oren attacked him. Now he would be in a stronger position to inhibit an impulsive person's behavior on behalf of the entire department rather than for the convenience of the director.

He also thought: "Why did I start this program anyway? Who else is getting snapped at like this?" Then he recalled the warning of the management consultant that it would take some time for men to tell the truth and really trust one another. During that time, it would become clear that some people could take it, and some could not. The director realized that this was a good way to find out who were the people that he could really count on to put their work before personal egotism. He began to enjoy the thoughts of measuring himself and Oren by these standards.

The director had decided that the program was worth what it would cost him in patience. He would have to suffer a fool gladly. This seemed to be a small price to pay in return for what he and others were learning about themselves, their promotional techniques, and their products through these open discussions.

Will I Be Rewarded?

The director perceives rewards to himself, his department, and his company through perseverance in the development of "peer review."

Why does the director think that he is being rewarded by keeping his temper, while the artist does not? The answer may lie in the different set of values. The director values loyalty to the objectives of his company, while the artist is primarily loyal to what *he* has produced. Oren likes what he does, and that is enough for him.

That's not enough for the director. He is pleased when other people like a program along with him. Much of his satisfaction comes out of the growth that he observes in those whom he has helped to train. In the case of peer review, he foresees more self-knowledge as men tell each other what they see in another man's performance. The staff will not only learn how their work is seen by others, but they will also learn something about themselves as they criticize or receive criticism. They had some practice on awareness of their reactions to others in the training seminars on management by objectives which preceded this promotional program.

Fortitude in itself is a reward. The director would think that he was "chicken" if he gave up objectives to which he had devoted many hours and a sizable amount of consultation fees, just because he had been personally attacked. One advantage of his telephone conversation with Carl was to feel that Carl and others supported the peer review. If Carl had reported that most of the staff were unable to cope with this kind of honest reporting, the director would have been wise to reduce his expectations and find out what was wrong. There would have been little reward in stubborn perseverance through a program that a staff was incapable of supporting.

We could express this in classical ethics by saying that prudence precedes fortitude. That is, we must count the cost of a program beforehand and then measure what it is costing us day by day. If staff morale is disintegrating, some changes must be made. But if the cost is personal discomfort, such as the director suffered, he will feel rewarded by continuing a program for the good of his whole department and thinking with his associate directors of ways to inhibit the destructive attitudes of one person in the department.

The director will probably be wise to check on his conclusions with more people than Carl. What do other staff members say about their trips together and their reports to one another? Prudence grows out of a realistic assessment that is shared by many people. When the director has put all of these comments together, he will know if fortitude will pay off or not. If morale and productivity are increased, this is probably more than enough to compensate for the uncomfortable moments that the director spent with Oren or the frustration that Oren will suffer when he is told to keep his temper.

Oren will have no successful retaliation upon the director if he is told that this discipline is being imposed for the good of the whole department. The director thought up a speech to Oren: "If you blow up in the face of other staff members in the same way that you did with me, no one will want to be on a team with you, and everybody will be careful of what they say before you in a staff meeting. So, I am telling you that our new program is not going to succeed unless you and everybody else can learn to listen. It's hard enough to give an accurate and fair evaluation of a colleague. It will be impossible when somebody acts like you have. Now, are you willing to make the effort to see that this program works, or do you really want to go back to the drawing board and stay there? Some guys do best when they just work by themselves, and maybe you are one of them." (He didn't get to deliver the speech that night; Oren didn't come in until after the director was asleep.)

This speech rehearsal brings justice into the picture.

The director will risk some inconvenience with a staff member on behalf of a worthy program, as he conceives it. He says to himself that he'll be vulnerable to additional attacks because he does not wish others to be attacked as he has been.

The pursuit of justice is a satisfying reward for continuing a program despite uncomfortable circumstances. In fact, without some sense of justice, fortitude would be futile. Stubborn perseverance in a program or in a particular type of behavior is not ethically rewarding by itself. We must be brave for the sake of something, not just to demonstrate to ourselves that we can "take it."

The director went through some of that struggle as he imagined and then laid aside words of personal vindictiveness toward Oren. If he had retaliated against a staff member just to show that he had the guts to stand up to him, he would have jeopardized the whole program through Oren's ability to twist retaliation into a sign that the director could not take the truth. But when he thought through the reasons why he should reply to Oren, justice became an important virtue. He would warn a self-indulgent staff member for the sake of others who were trying to be honest with him.

Can I Be Cheerful?

It is obvious that the director had a good deal of self-confidence in his first encounter with Oren. He was not easily shaken by the attack, asked for identification of his critics and the substance of their remarks. He was strong enough to learn willingly from enemies. Self-assurance increases our sense of endurance under attack. For one thing we can look openly at the cause of our problem, like the director who was asking where the criticism came from. If he had not felt sure of himself, his defenses would have risen, and he would have sought to justify himself before he knew what the real charges were and where they started.

This kind of assurance is not the same as arrogance. It is a temperate knowledge of ourselves. That is, we know by experience what kind of reactions people usually have to us and have tested our perception against those of others. For example, the director told me: "I felt myself getting angry when that fellow cursed me and talked about the poor job that I had done. I knew that I had not done that badly. Then I thought, this is the first time that a staff member had insulted me in years. I . . . guess that's what stopped me from blasting him. I began to wonder what was wrong with this guy and thought that I should check it out with his supervisor before I did anything. I know that I ramble sometimes, like he says, but I can take that criticism, and I usually can criticize others without them getting hostile, like he did."

"How did you decide that this is the way you are?" I asked. He replied: "When you have been in advertising for twenty years, you learn to look at your proposals and products from every angle—that includes some criticisms of the pet way that you do things. You don't succeed if you have a chip on your shoulder or some precious product that you must protect. People have told me many times that I hit them hard, but they don't think that I am trying to annihilate them. They soon realize that I will tell them what I think and where they stand with me, and that's that. They don't have to worry about me getting them, unless there's somebody like this guy Oren."

The director is not only aware of how he has related to people in the past, he also has some ideas of what will happen in the future. He was determined that the staff would continue to be honest with each other in the evaluation of a new program. He considered Oren to be a "special case" that would have to be settled on an individual basis. He was not in despair about the prospects of management by objectives and was not cynical about all staff members because of one person's hostility.

This sense of hope saw him through a strenuous session with Oren and Carl when the three were together after the promotional tour.

> **Director:** "Oren, I wanted to tell you that Carl and I see a threat to our program in the reaction that you have to criticism. If you blow up with other members of the staff in the way that you blow up with us, they are not going to tell you what they think about your part in this project. They'll just clam-up and isolate you. Or if you attack them the way that you have attacked me, they'll get angry, and we will have a fight on our hands. That won't help communication either."
>
> **Oren:** "Why are you telling me this here in Carl's presence, here in his office? It sounds like I am on trial or something."
>
> **Director:** "I am telling you to control your temper and to look at your performance with the rest of the staff rather than being touchy and acting as though we were going to do you in."

Oren: "Oh, *you* want to tell me exactly what you think about me, but you don't want me to say a word. It's all a one-way street. Is that it?"

Carl: "It will be a one-way if you try to put down anybody who evaluates your work when they are on your team."

Oren: "Sure, sure, I am the bad boy who has to take it. You are the good guys who always dish it out. Now that I tell the boss what I think, I get called on the carpet."

Director: "You can say what you think without insulting people. I think that I 'dish it out' without degrading anybody. So does Carl. And I think that most of our team can do the same. So how about you?"

Oren: "You really want to know what I think? I think that when you want to get a guy, you can think of reasons to get him. Now you've thought up one on me—"

Carl: "Now take it easy, I trust—"

Oren: [Interrupting] "Trust! Ha! The only thing that I can trust from this man is that he will use his power to get somebody that he does not like. You can't run a business without trust."

Director: "I don't know, I don't know. I don't think we are working on the problem of trust right now. Come to think of it, I haven't seen a great deal of trust in organizations anyway, at least not from where I sit. I don't think that I could expect you to trust me, and I don't expect that of some other people."

Oren: "Well, that's probably the reason you have gotten up to where you are. Being trusted doesn't matter much to you."

Director: "Since I am in this position, I have a question for you. If I were out to get you, why would I have troubled myself to go through a hot discussion with you on the tour and take time to talk with you now? If I wanted to get you, would it not have been easier for me to have filed a report with Carl and let him take care of it?"

Oren: "Well, then what do you want out of me? Why don't you tell me what you require? You're the boss. You can say it."

Director: "I will. Keep your temper and stop insulting people who try to tell you how to improve your performance."

Oren: "Is that it? [Director and Carl nod.] Well, thank you very much! Now if you gentlemen do not mind I will go back to my work." [The "gentlemen" nod again, and Oren walks out of the office.]

Carl: "That was OK, Ted. You kept it at the level of what was needed by our staff and didn't let him get to you personally."

Director: "What a job! That guy wears you out. Does he ever learn anything from anybody else?"

Carl: "Not much. He does what he does well, and that's it. I don't know if he will make it on these promotion teams."

Director: "Well, he's certainly not making it

with me. Let's see what happens when everybody reports in our next staff meeting."

Between that conversation and the weekly staff meeting, Ted was a happy man. He was relaxed on the golf course, attentive to his wife, cheerful in his greetings to secretaries. As he said to me later: "Why was I feeling so good? I guess it was a good feeling about making a decision. I guess you never really commit yourself to a program until there is some problem to solve and you have to make a tough decision. Well, I went through the wringer with this guy, and I felt better about the whole thing that we were trying to do. I saw that the program was not only going to sharpen up our promotional packages, but it also brought to the surface some of the bad apples that had been lying in the bottom of the barrel."

> **Southard:** "Ted, the old saying is that a bad apple will spoil the whole barrel."
>
> **Director:** "Yeah, that's right. Oren did try to poison the well some after our meeting, and he made some insinuating remarks in staff about the level of trust around here and how people had to be careful what they would say or they would be cut down. When some other people asked him just what he had in mind, he said that he had rather not say here in open meeting. When they pushed him, he said that it was not easy to be on a team with the boss. Another man spoke up and said that he didn't think that that

was any problem. I was aggressive and hard to stop, but I could be stopped. He gave an example of his work on a previous team with me. He said that I eventually listened to him and changed the way that I was presenting our product because of what he said. People asked how I had presented myself, and I told them. Then we moved on to a discussion of how some other people were presenting their packages of material. We never got back to Oren, and he just sat there with a stern look on his face for the rest of the meeting."

Southard: "So you still feel cheerful?"

Director: "Yeah, even more so. After that meeting, Carl said that he had really wondered if I would carry through on this team approach. He had seen some other managers try it in other departments, and they gave it up. He went on to say that he did not mean to say that I should be stubborn and do it if there was lots of opposition, but he did want to see if I still had the guts to stay with something even when there was some criticism."

Southard: "So now you think that the program is shaping up to your satisfaction?" [I was wondering if there was any further need for a consultant.]

Director: "Well, I think it is just a matter of staying with it. I kicked it off, then people grabbed hold and began to move. And now I guess they want to know if I am going to take their reports seriously. Will I back up the changes they make in our advertising of a particular product and will I hold to that up the line? The answer is yes." [He smiles]

I was especially impressed with the cheerfulness of this manager's manner. He had shown patience with an employee, courage in inhibiting a threat to open communications, aggressiveness in moving ahead with a project in which he had much hope.

Perhaps he did not harm Oren because he was hopeful that the program would succeed. If he had given way to his irritation with this belligerent subordinate, it might have thrown a bad light upon the spirit of the program and his leadership of it. Since the program was more important than the defensive attitudes of any one employee, the director endured this attack cheerfully. He didn't act as though he enjoyed things when he was being insulted, but his general good humor was sustained. He was confident of himself, but did not take himself so seriously that he could not endure hostility with patience. He also had enough respect for the opinions of others to get some cues from Carl as to the best way of responding to Oren. Without this, he might have turned the discipline of Oren's communication problem, which was an act for the entire organization, into a personal fight between superior and subordinate. It seems that this is what Oren had hoped for, but he was disappointed.

Why did Oren not succeed in his attempts to intimidate Ted, to make him feel guilty and subsequently leave him alone? The answer seems to be Ted's trust in something beyond himself. With a little help from Carl, Ted thought first about his responsibilities as the leader of a program that would benefit individuals and his agency. He had to give some thought to what type of person he was and how he was being treated, but that was not so much on his mind that he could be trapped into imprudent rage by insolent behavior. He was not even led into cynicism, which could also have killed the spirit of the program.

When our courage is based upon something beyond our own dignity, we are in less danger of losing it. We can look with an open mind at the range of problems before us and respond with good humor to some of our difficulties because we have counted the cost of this style of management and are rewarded by a sense of loyalty to our ideals. It is this inner conviction of courage that allows us to identify an attack, consider alternatives, and take action that can turn bad consequences into profit for good decisions.

What are these values that cause us to feel "profited" despite provocation? There must be some inner compass that guides a man toward integrity despite the diversions of intimidation, insult, inequalities, improper influence. When we really want to know what is going on inside the boss's mind, we have to ask the question of our next chapter: "What do I live for?"

6

What Do I Live For?

When 2,800 businessmen defined their basic goals and aspirations on an American Management Association questionnaire, their first priorities were domestic tranquility, continued good health, basic job and financial security.[1] The basic objectives of executives are personal, private, or family-centered. The accumulation of wealth or the attainment of status in the community are secondary. And, among respondents under 30 years of age, the gradual perfection of religious faith is held up as a worthy life's aim.

Do you agree with these findings? If you're satisfied with your personal and professional progress, you probably will. The satisfied businessmen in the survey held religious value in higher esteem, exalted qualities of integrity above qualities of "personality," felt the continuing influence of parental ideals.

---

[1] Dale Tarnowieski, "The Changing Success Ethic," New York: AMACOM, 1973.

In contrast, less satisfied businessmen had different concepts of success from parents, believed that personal contacts were the most important factor in job achievement, placed high value on occupational status and authority.[2]

The Way Beyond Wealth

Thirty-four percent of the respondents said that success increasingly represents the realization of goals and aspirations that may have little to do with career advancement. If this is so, what are the values that really matter to an executive?

An answer to that question may be found in a survey of the topics that excite the most interest today:

- **Conformity vs non-conformity**
- **Dependence vs equality of the sexes**
- **Self-assertion vs self-despair**
- **Collectivism vs private ownership**
- **Rugged individualism vs interpersonal relationships**

Do you see how the ordering of these topics conforms to the stages of personality development and interests?

Conformity vs nonconformity is an issue of early adolescence. This is the time of rebellion against parental or social norms, a day of questioning and searching. Most of us move through that necessary stage to some balance between autonomy and acculturation. Like the JC who heard the secretary's remarks about his shoes, we may conform in dress or style because that's not really important to us.

---

[2] *ibid.,* p. 3.

But some people are still fighting as adults the battles of parent and child. They test the company or their supervisors by conformity/nonconformity in dress, customs, language, regulations. Some are continually testing the limits—how much can they get away with? Others are at the opposite extreme of caution in all things—what do superiors expect?

A preoccupation with conformity or nonconformity makes a poor manager. If your values are here, you're a delayed adolescent.

Other managers are caught up in a topic that could be an extension of the conformity question. It's the problem of sexual equality. Usually we settle that issue about the time of marriage and either accept traditional roles of husband and wife or the newer opportunities of equality in all things. Now, the equalitarian position shows more adaptability to modern life, but I would not accuse a traditionalist of immaturity. My point is that continual contest about this topic either way is immature. If the presence or absence of female supervisors bugs you more than any other topic of the day, you're still thinking like a bridegroom. An eternal contest between the sexes is not the deepest issue with which mature people are concerned. We are to think beyond sex, race, religious affiliation to the questions of competence, loyalty, trust, grace, and truthfulness in personal relationships.

Executives' wives noted the immaturity of some executives in their great concern for masculine dominance. They were men who thought that managers should be tough, speak rough, have all the answers. The women suspected that this bravado was a smoke screen for feelings of personal inadequacy.

What about personal inadequacy? That's the next stage of maturity, the question of self-assertion vs despair. It appears from the AMA questionnaire of Tarnowieski that many managers are hung up at that level of development. There is overwhelming agreement in the questionnaire returns that a dynamic personality, the ability to sell oneself, is a more important attribute in organizations than a reputation for honesty or firm principles.[3] Maybe this is just an assessment of where the organization is, but I suspect that it is also, or more so a reflection of what the businessman expects of himself. Tarnowieski also notes the tragic end of self-assertiveness in Arthur Miller's play, *Death of a Salesman*. The "personality" ethic, by itself, loses meaning with every year of life.

Certainly it is true that JC's are aggressive and assured of success. We expect this of young men. And, as I pointed out in earlier chapters, self-respect and a tested sense of worth are necessary for realistic and enduring ethical decisions. But the assumption is that self-assurance goes beyond youthful exuberance to a more deliberative view of the world. We cannot always project inexhaustable enthusiasm. The wise man begins early to ease up on his expectations, to decide how to get the most within his limits, to set goals that are attainable within a reasonable period of time. In short, a mature person prepares for death.

This sounds morbid, or is it? It can be, when a middle-aged man has his first heart attack and says to me: "Why am I in bed while my competitors, who lie and cheat, steal my customers?" If you've built your life around "hitting the competition hard," there's nothing but despair

---

[3] *ibid.*, p. 29.

when you're told to take it easy for six months—or else.

Of course you could learn from the jolting experience of a close brush with death or financial disaster. When I made a hospital visit to a fifty-year-old executive he told me: "Why didn't you tell me last year that I was going to drive myself into a heart attack? I should have known that this was coming. I have been abusing my body for years." Then he smiled and said: "Of course you could not have told me, and no one else could have told me. It had to happen before I would accept any limitations. I've decided that I ran so hard because I never really had time for any friends. If I had thought about friends, I wouldn't have been so busy charming everyone that I met. When I get out of this place, I'm going to try and develop some enduring relationships."

You can accumulate wealth in twenty years of acting like a zestful junior executive. But at about forty-five or fifty, the shallowness of self-assertion begins to show itself. Then you either keep trying with diminishing "personality" reserves, or you give in to despair and cynicism.

There's a time around twenty-five or thirty when we really do not know our own strength. We can get up early, beat the competition, play golf, work late into the night, and spend the weekend playing with the kids. The question is, will you continue to expect that of yourself at fifty and sixty, or will you begin to cultivate some values that do not depend upon physical and emotional energy?

Middle-aged businessmen have spent much energy on the question of collectivism versus private ownership. This is a value-ladened question that has turned some after-dinner conversations into shouting matches. The issues are certainly worth a good deal of time and thought, for they involve the security and happiness of many persons for whom we are responsible. But the moral problem is that some men make collectivism versus private ownership the ultimate test of fellowship and acceptance. A public official stated the problem this way: "I try to find out what some of these businessmen have against our publicly financed health care and delivery systems. They are men of the world who understand organization, but all they see in these health insurance programs is socialism. They don't suggest any alternatives and they don't seem to be really concerned about the problem of people who lack care. I don't understand this, because they are good men. But they really cannot think through this subject."

The same speech could be made by some exponents of private enterprise about some advocates of collectivism. Either side sees this issue as *the* most important one in the world today. It certainly is important, and it commands the best minds and experience of business and government to solve. But is it the most basic issue, the question that causes you to decide who will be your friend or your enemy? When I put the question this way to a wise executive, he laughed and replied: "Now don't try to catch me in a trap where I will say that *things* are more important than *people*. I think that property is important, and that it can be used to help people. But I am not going to say that a man's views on the control and distribution of property comes before anything else in my relationship to him."

The executive's emphasis upon persons is the basis of all the questions that we have raised in this book. It is the foundation upon which we order all of the other values that we have just discussed in this chapter.[4] The basic ethical question is what do I think about myself and what do I think about other people? Character and integrity come before views on the distribution of property, the enthusiasm of our salesmanship, our approval or disapproval of women's rights and our conformity or nonconformity to custom.

When Chester Barnard and others talk about the "breadth of morality" upon which executive leadership rests, I think of this progressive ordering of values that begins with personal relationships. This is the most profound basis of life upon which we may judge all of the other issues that come to us in the office, the home, and society.

We can illustrate the basic nature of the value of persons by considering the troublesome questions of race, sex, and age. Many managers are troubled by the injustice that may occur when a woman or a black person is advanced in management just because they fit the category of "minority." Does the person have the necessary competence and maturity for this position? What is to be said about white men who have the maturity and competence for advancement, but who are not preferred? Although questions about sex and race are important in a scale of values, they are not the most important. The basic question is, do I have respect for this person as one who can do the job to which I promote him or her? If the answer is yes, we must also consider the question of how other persons will feel about this promotion. We have to go beyond the categories of sex and race to make a decision that will support the person

---

[4] For further discussion of these values, see the book from which I drew my discussion of them: *The Struggle of the Soul,* by Lewis Sherill (New York: The Macmillian Company, 1951), Chapter 5.

who is upgraded and strengthen his relationships to others in the office or plant.

The same is true for discussion about age. On the one hand, we perpetuate injustice to make an exception for a fifty-five-year-old man who is elevated beyond his capacities. As the Jaycees observed in one seminar, you cannot keep a man in a position just because he has seniority. You must think of the place where he can be most effective and you must also think of the other persons with whom he works.

The Basis of Belief

Executives have also said that they feel better about themselves when their actions and attitudes show courage, consistency, temperance, justice. When we know ourselves and practice self-control, it is a value both to our own inner feelings and to our working relationships.

We have yet to delve into the most basic question, why are we made in such a way that satisfactions come through ethical encounters? O. A. Ohmann addressed this question when he wrote in the *Harvard Business Review* that men are looking for "sky hooks." He believed that workers have a fine sensitivity to spiritual qualities and want to work for a boss who believes in something and in whom they can believe. The administrator can set the climate within which values do or do not become working realities. The successful executive is one who believes that the world was created by God who holds men ultimately responsible to him.[5]

An executive is moral because of what he believes about the world. The assertion of Mr. Ohmann is borne out in

---

[5] O. A. Ohmann "Sky Hooks" *Harvard Business Review,* January-February, 1970, pp. 4-20.

many executive conferences. It begins in statements from Junior Chamber of Commerce men that they cannot think of anyone going up the corporation ladder just because he knows the bosses' weaknesses. Early in business, they show a conviction that the world is moral, and that the only lasting satisfactions come from a reliance upon this reality.

The same conviction is stated more earnestly by the wives of senior executives, who say that the world is moral and those who are ethical will be happier and more successful. When asked for the basis of this belief, they refer to their personal experiences with their husband and to a theological statement, "This is God's will." One said: "I think that my husband's patience and ability to relate to people as people is a part of his Christian convictions. He believes that this is the way that he is *supposed* to act. Oh, maybe it doesn't sound quite right that way. It isn't that he acts this way because others expect it of him; it's because he thinks that this is what his religion has taught him, and since he really does care for people, it's quite consistent. Sometimes I think that his impatience with people has to be curbed by his convictions. He has very high expectations of himself and thinks the same of others. When they disappoint him, he might be hard to get along with if it were not for the things that he believes in."

Senior executives make some of the same statements. They think of virtue as the natural result of a man's knowledge of the world as it is. From their point of view, a man who practices deception in business or who cheats on his wife is unrealistic. He has not really figured out the way that the world is made. They acknowledge the way in which some men get ahead for a short period of time through shady practices, but they doubt that many executives can last in a moral limbo, and they do not think that any person is really satisfied with himself under these conditions.

Why this conviction that it is realistic to do right? For an answer to that question we can look again at the research of Milton Rokeach in *The Open and Closed Mind*. He found that dogmatic persons view the world as a very threatening place. Chronic anxiety has plagued these persons from childhood. It is difficult for them to accept the views of others unless the view is related to some fixed authority. There are many prejudices in these persons and little concern for those who do not share their opinions.

In contrast, people who see the world as a good place are open to the opinion of others, secure in their own convictions, able to see the good and bad in fathers, mothers, and others while they still maintain good relationships.

The "closed-minded" people cling to religious values for convenience. This gives them security in the midst of change. The "open-minded" group become more religious as years pass by, and they develop a deeper consciousness of God's work in the world and in their own lives.[6]

In theological terms, we could say that a child first experiences love when he feels the affection of his parents. As he grows toward maturity, they provide him with both acceptance and frustration. He is loved as their child, but he is also taught to respect the convictions and convenience of others. By the time that this person accepts adult responsibility, he has solid evidences that God cares for him and a conviction that he should care for others. There is no threat in this. It is only the working out of the way

---

[6] Milton Rokeach, *The Open and Closed Mind,* pp. 336-342.

that things ought to be. It is a sense of God's purposes for the lives of men.

This unshakable sense of God's purpose for His world is the fountainhead of morality. It only seems natural to act with virtue when you know that this is the reason for our creation. We are only imitating our Creator when we love one another.

At the same time, this love can be made real through justice in the world. The executive who has a sense of inner peace through his knowledge of God is able to make discriminating judgments that bring satisfactions to himself and others. In contrast, the person who is beset by chronic anxieties will make decisions with a blurred vision. His defenses are so high that he cannot see the whole picture, and his view of God is as narrow as his view of the world.

How shall we relate to those who view the world as a threatening place? If they can be open about the terror that they experienced in childhood or the many embarrassments of early struggles in the Depression, we can often rationalize their pushing, gouging, greedy ways. We do not want them in the executive suite, but we can do business with them because we know why they are the way they are, and they seem to know this also. We have more difficulty with the man who talks about the goodness of God but lives as though God has no power in the world. This is the hypocrite, the man who feels that the hand of every man is against him, but that God is on his side. We wonder how this man can say that he loves God when he does not love his fellowman.

The hypocrite is always on the defensive against God and man. He cannot really believe that God has made a good world, and that He will sustain those who are gracious.

Our only choice is to relate to the man's actions rather than to his words. We can maintain an honest relationship with these people by establishing relationships based on their distrust of everything that we say and do. So long as we are not misled by their religious language, there is no great problem. We maintain a minimum of contact, under specified conditions, with little or no personal involvement. These people have been hurt so often when they were young and vulnerable that they are instinctively suspicious of anyone who tries to be kind to them as adults. Their views of the world may not be the same as yours.

Choosing Between Better and Best

When I talk about God's will and a secure view of the world, I am not saying that all moral decisions are automatically solved. It is one thing to affirm that God has made a good world in which we are to live in love with our brethren. It is another thing to choose what is best for us and our brethren. This is especially difficult when we are choosing between the good and the best, or when it seems that two goals are equally deserving and only one of them can be accomplished. What do we do then?

The answer is a structuring of priorities such as we have tried to do in this chapter. For example, it is clear, at least from the AMA questionnaire, that most businessmen would place family concerns first, job satisfaction second, and the accumulation of wealth third.

But how do we know what priority is involved now, and

what is the process through which we make a decision and carry it out? This is the reason for our questions, chapter by chapter, on who we are, how we are responsible for others, and what are the consequences.

A Specific Example

Mr. Reynolds needed to ask himself all of these questions when he wanted to dissolve a partnership with his brother. Mr. Reynolds felt that it was not fair to him and his family to do seventy-five percent of the work and receive only fifty percent of the income from the business. How was he going to tell his brother that he wanted to dissolve their equal partnership in a business that had been established by their father?

When Mr. Reynolds talked over the problem with his wife, he found a sympathetic listener but no solution. At least he learned from talking with her that he was irritable with her and preoccupied before the children. Something had to be done if he was going to enjoy his family as he had in the past. Then his wife reminded him that a college classmate, who had gone into the field of personnel work, had recently bought a business in their section of town. Why not talk to this friend who had training and experience in counseling people about decisions? So Mr. Reynolds called his classmate and took him out to lunch.

After lunch at the club, the two men took a little stroll around the golf course. Mr. Reynolds explained that his brother had plenty of ability, but he never seemed to apply himself. He used to drink a lot, and he had been sulky in childhood. Now he did what he wanted to. If a buyer came in to see him, and he was out playing golf, the appointment was just missed.

Mr. Reynolds: "I guess I don't like the idea of supporting two families when he should be taking care of his end of the load."

Friend: "Well, if this is getting so close to you that it goes home with you, something ought to be done—"

Mr. Reynolds: [Interrupting] "If we break up this company, what will happen to Pete [older brother]? He might go to pieces. He doesn't know what hard work is. He is over fifty and might not get another job. It's tough, I know, but I don't want to do anything that's going to pull him apart."

Friend: "Has this been rocking along for years? You have never mentioned anything like this to me before."

Mr. Reynolds: "I guess it would have rocked along for years and years if we hadn't lost our lease for the office. We've had to move over to the bank building, and it cost us some money. Then, if we stay in this new location, we must sign a five-year lease. So, I figured it was time for me to say something or get hold of myself."

Friend: "So now is the time."

Mr. Reynolds: "Yeah, and I tell myself that it might not be so bad. After all, Pete is a big talker and has lots of friends in town. He sure spends enough time in talking with those friends, but [pause] he has sometimes talked about going into politics, and I think that is what he ought to do. He really has a good mind and reads alot in the evenings. You know, Judge Potter is going to retire next year, and I had thought that Pete would be an excellent man for that position. [Pause.] And then, there is another thing. In all fairness to my brother, he has done some things for the business that I didn't do. He meets people easily, and they like him. That has brought us business. Maybe I get too tied up with things and take them too seriously. Sometimes he tells me so. But then, I want to take this decision seriously. I don't want to do anything that's going to hurt my brother. At the same time, I don't want my family to suffer."

Friend: "Say, are you afraid of Pete?"

Mr. Reynolds: "No, I'm more afraid of what might happen to me. I mean I get all tied up in these things. I thought last year that maybe I should just do away with myself. That's a terrible idea, but I just did not know where to turn. If I dissolve this partnership, I'll be much better off financially. I'll get along better with my family. I know that my brother has no right to use me up. I guess I just need to talk this out with somebody to be sure in my own mind that I am doing the right thing."

Mr. Reynolds is beginning to ask one of the questions

about justice: "To whom am I responsible?" He knows that he has obligations from the past to his brother, and he has some in the present to his own family. There may be others that he has not yet discussed. When he has finished his conversations, he should know to whom he is *most* responsible.

"What happens when I'm involved?" is another question that is beginning to appear. He now realizes that there is much less in the partnership for him than there was in the past. He also realizes that some of his feelings of frustration are beginning to show in his own family. Now he is trying to see himself in action. The big question for the future will be: "Is he really strong enough to make a decision that may hurt somebody?"

After giving these questions some thought, Mr. Reynolds was pleased to find that he and his friend were at the same civic club, one as a regular member and the other as a visitor. Afterwards, Mr. Reynolds walked back to the car with his friend, and they talked some more about the way in which he would dissolve the partnership. It was a complicated procedure that he did not discuss in detail, but it was clear that he had spent much time in arranging things so that the disposition would be equitable. The friend commented that Reynolds seemed to be businesslike and at the same time fair in dealings with his brother.

Mr. Reynolds: "Yes, that's the same thing that Mother told me when I talked with her. I had really felt that I should tell her something about the business since she had stock in it, left by my father. I told her that this was a business problem, not a personal problem. She said that I had done well to stay in the business with Pete since my father died. She felt that my brother was selfish, always had been, and always would be. She loves him, but she says that she might as well tell me that Pete is not going to change. Well, I felt better after talking with her. She seemed to approve of what I was doing. She didn't say that I was disloyal to my father, or anything like that. It made me more determined to do the right thing and not hurt my own family anymore."

Friend: "Does your wife think that you are still hurting the family—or is this just your idea?"

Mr. Reynolds: "Well, the wife pointed out to me last night that I am worrying too much about this. She said that we could go on like we are so far as she is concerned, but that it would be hard on me, and she can see it. She thinks that Pete can stand on his own feet and make his own decisions. Well, I think I should do something now. Business is slow right now, and it's a good time to set things in order."

Friend: "You don't think that things will get any better?"

Mr. Reynolds: "They will not. Last week when business was slow, and we needed to make as many contacts as we could, Pete spent most of the week over in the stockbroker's office planning his own financial improvement. He really likes to sit there and look at the board and see how much he has made on his own private investments. I am stuck in the office and can't get out to see the customers that we need to see. I tell you if I don't make a clean break now, I will be a coward."

Now Mr. Reynolds is getting into the questions of our fourth chapter: "When and How Do I Act?" He has decided to be honest with himself. If he continues the way he has been, he is taking inappropriate responsibility for his brother. He knows from his mother and probably from his wife that the brother can take care of himself. So is it not time for him to be frank with his brother?

Certainly he has given enough thought to the exact way in which financial arrangements are to be made. It seemed clear to his friend that the action was not motivated by any sense of revenge against the brother, since the distribution of assets seemed to be fair and equitable. It now seems that Mr. Reynolds has set a good time for his action. He should take action during a slack season when there is time for the brothers to work out their negotiations. Also, Mr. Reynolds is beginning to realize that the pressure is building up in him to take some action before he gets too irritable and is disagreeable with Pete.

But Mr. Reynolds still has some difficulty with the question of consequences. He began to have some severe doubts about himself, which drove him to go by the office of his friend late one afternoon. The friend noticed that Mr. Reynolds had a cold. He sniffed and coughed during the conversations. He did not look very well.

Friend: "Well, has there been some change in your thinking?"

Mr. Reynolds: "I'm not sure I can trust my thinking, but I decided that I need to take the risk. I have got to do this for myself. Of course I know I am passing judgment on my brother. I know this is not right. All I can say is that I would not change a thing if I thought it would be best for him and for me, but I am more than ever convinced that it is no good for either of us to go on this way. Maybe he was just born this way."

Friend: "So what happens now?"

Mr. Reynolds: Well, it is time for me to talk with my brother. There is no use in putting this off any longer. If I don't, I will begin to resent him more than I do now and that will make things worse."

Friend: "OK. It seems to me that we have talked enough about this. After you talk with Pete, let me know how things come out."

It's fortunate that Mr. Reynolds had a friend who knew how to respond to him in a way that would lead toward action. Without this, Mr. Reynolds might have been like many other executives who keep putting off the decisions that will hurt someone. We are especially prone to do this when there are complicating circumstances such as family ties. If Mr. Reynolds had not had that someone to keep him steady, the process of moral decision making might have been aborted. But as it is, there is a brief hesitation and then another move toward resolution of the problem.

Mr. Reynolds called his friend three weeks later and

really sounded much better over the telephone. He invited Mr. Reynolds to come over about five o'clock.

When Mr. Reynolds came in, he looked relieved. He could hardly wait to tell his friend that "a major breakthrough had occurred" in the relationship to the brother.

Mr. Reynolds: "It was a week ago today. I just sat down and told him that we had been in the partnership long enough. I was anxious to be on my own. I had worked things out in my own mind and felt that it could be done fairly for both of us."

Friend: "So now it has been done. Sounds good. How did your brother take it?"

Mr. Reynolds: "Like a man. [Smiles.] I guess I was too worried about things. I always said that my brother had lots of ability, and I guess I should have given him credit for thinking things through. Anyway, he just asked how I was thinking of rearranging things, and I showed him what I had written out. He had some good ideas. He thought that we could change things so that I would be independent, but we still could share some things together and save expenses. For example, we could sign the lease in this new office for the next five years and share the expenses. Since neither of us have too much dictation, we could also write up a contract to share expenses for the same stenographer. She knows both of us and how we do our work, and he thought that we could keep the same name on the firm, even though we kept separate accounts. We agreed on it, shook hands and have set a date for the formal separation in about three months."

Friend: "Well, you certainly seem relieved and your brother seems to think this will work out for the good of all concerned."

Mr. Reynolds: "Yes, it is a relief and I am glad that he took it the way that he did. And, like I said, he had some good things to say. I had not realized that we could still work together while he made his money, and I made mine. But, I see now that it can be done. Anyway, my part of the business is going great now, and that may make me feel better. It's always good to have plenty of calls and to see that we are on the upswing. It happens every fall, but of course I am never real sure about it."

Friend: "Things look good right now. I tell you what. I'll be seeing you at the club every couple of weeks, and if there is any hitch in your plans, give me the high sign. We can get together if something should develop."

Mr. Reynolds: "Thanks, it's been good to have somebody listen while I cleared this up in my own mind. Maybe I overestimated my importance to my brother. Looks like he is going to do O.K. Maybe *I'm* the one who will be shaky."

Friend: "Well, I doubt it. You always work hard and have a good reputation. Besides, nothing has really happened between you and your brother. You just have some things out in the open, and both of you are glad about it. So far as anybody in the community is concerned, things are going along as they were in the company. And, as far as I am concerned, what you have talked about will stay right here in this office."

It seems as though Mr. Reynolds chose the right kind of responsibility. He drew back from trying to take care of his brother's life and emphasized his own life and his family's. In doing so, he freed himself from annoyance with his brother and found that his brother could take care of himself. As Mr. Reynolds admits, he may have worried too much about his importance to his brother.

In considering the consequences, Mr. Reynolds is pleased. He had thought that the cost might have been heavy in the beginning, but this did not prove to be the case. For one thing, his mother supported him rather than rebuking him. For another, he realized that his brother could take care of himself. He did not have to feel a great load of responsibility. Sure enough, the brother came up with some good suggestions as the partnership was dissolved. It seems that the real cost to Mr. Reynolds was some hard work on himself. He had to think through what was most important in his life right now, and he had to think about the way he was acting around people who were significant to him. Most of all, he had to get rid of some of his old feelings of relying on his brother.

In the end, Mr. Reynolds has obtained more of a reward than he had really looked for. He had gone into this decision with the feeling that he would be rewarded by peace of mind and happiness with his family. This was the minimal satisfaction. As it turned out, he also gained approval from his mother and respect from his brother.

Can I Make Good Decisions?

We may not all be fortunate enough to have an understanding friend, and we may not move through our moral decisions with the good results that Mr. Reynolds enjoyed, but we will probably need to ask some of the same questions if we are going to find the right answers. We will need a thorough knowledge of ourselves when we get involved in an ethical issue. We will need to know the demands that we must realistically meet. We must be frank with others and sensitive to the timing of our actions. And we must count the cost of the value decisions upon which our character is based.

Like Mr. Reynolds, it will take some courage. Sometimes we need instantaneous resoluteness to preserve justice. At other times, as in this case, there will be a long and painful process of decision making. Whatever the timing, the basic ingredients of a moral decision will still be the classic virtues of temperance, prudence, justice, and bravery. These are the ingredients of an ethical executive who is building a strong company. As Mr. Ohmann said in a retrospective commentary fifteen years after his first writing of "Sky Hooks," the great executives that he had known were those who had something deep inside that supported them. It was something ultimate and personal that went beyond reason and gave them calm and confident attitudes.[7]

---

[7] O. A. Ohmann, "Sky Hooks," *Harvard Business Review,* January-February 1970, p. 6.

7
Do I Believe in Justice?

That which is ultimate and personal in our lives is most clearly revealed when there is some question of justice for *us*. When we are under the stress of job security or a threat to our professional reputation, we show what we believe about God and the world. Some managers remain calm and confident because they really believe that the world was created good and that evil has no ultimate triumph. Others become distrustful and hopeless because they are convinced that the world sets every man against his brother and God delivers only those who help themselves.

Let's consider a typical case of interpersonal difficulty that reveals a young executive's character under stress. It's included in this volume to show that "goodness" doesn't always triumph—in one place.

. . .

Dr. Pinchney was on his way to a Medical Society meeting when he learned that his work was in danger. He was driving with Dr. Roth, a sixty-year-old professor of physiology in the Medical School. Dr. Pinchney is a thirty-five-year-old assistant professor of anatomy.

Dr. Roth: "I made a special point of asking to drive to this meeting with you. I want to ask what is going on between you and Dr. Mann." [Dr. Mann is the senior professor of anatomy who has been with the Medical School for twenty years.] "You have really shaken him up, and he is talking about you with me and other senior members of the faculty."

Dr. Pinchney: "Well, we have had some conflicts about students, but I thought that we had talked those out."

Dr. Roth: "No, no. This is much more personal. He says that you do not know your subject and that your teaching is 'sloppy.' He says that he has tried to warn you about this, but that you argue with him. He says that he has lost confidence in you as a younger colleague and that he will recommend to the dean that you not be given tenure at the end of this year. You look like you have not heard any of this before."

Dr. Pinchney: "No. It hits me like ice water. I don't know how to answer."

Dr. Roth: "You will need to find some answer in a month or Dr. Mann will have completed his campaign, and you will not have tenure. So, you need to work this out with him or talk it out with some of us. Personally, I think you are a good man and should be retained, but it will take some work to do that. You have made a powerful enemy. I should tell you that Charles [Dr. Mann] talks to me frequently about things, and has talked more about you than anything else in the past three months. You have really stirred him up."

Dr. Pinchney: "I am sorry to hear this. Dr. Mann was very helpful to me last year. I know that something has happened, but I don't know what it is. Like I said, there have been disagreements about the way we teach students, but [pause] . . ."

Dr. Ross: "Well, he thinks you are insensitive to him. He has tried to teach you this year as he did last year, and he says that you don't listen to him anymore. In fact, to just tell you all of it, he thinks you are stirring up the students against him."

Dr. Pinchney: "How could I do that? He is like God to most of those freshmen!"

Dr. Roth: "That's the problem. He's not God to you. In some way you have let the students know that. So now they are questioning some of his pronouncements. He can't stand that. You ought to know that."

Dr. Pinchney: "Well, I guess I should, but I guess I did not know it enough. I respect his opinions and his experience and all that, but I do have my own judgments about some of the explanations that he gives."

Dr. Roth: "Well, I suggest that you talk to him about this if you can. Maybe it can be worked out. But, when you talk to him, don't mention my name. He's a dangerous man when he thinks he's being attacked. I want to keep the lines of communication open with him. If he thinks that I am advising you, he'll turn on both of us."

A week later, Dr. Roth saw Dr. Pinchney on the way from the Medical School to a cafeteria a block away. As they walked along, Dr. Roth commented:

Dr. Roth: "Well, you must have seen Charles. He was very high in praise of you this morning. He told me that you had talked to him like a man and admitted that you did not listen to him as you should."

Dr. Pinchney: "That wasn't what I said. I said I would try to hear his point better and hope that he would listen more carefully to mine. I meant that we would try to understand each other better. I did not mean that I would agree with what he said."

Dr. Roth: "Easy, easy. I can understand what you tried to say, but Charles is going to understand it in his way. He has been number one for a long time and doesn't think he is wrong. I know it's hard to swallow, but you'll have to humble yourself for a while to get along with him. Think you can stand that?"

Dr. Pinchney: "Well, I'll see."

Two days later a number of freshmen gathered for an introduction to medicine seminar. Dr. Pinchney led the discussion and Dr. Mann and a professor of biochemistry contributed. In discussing the management of a patient, Dr. Pinchney asked a student for an opinion. The answer was agreeable to Dr. Pinchney, but not to Dr. Mann.

Dr. Mann: "No, young man, you are taking too much responsibility there. You should have made a referral."

Student: "But, sir, I'm on a state scholarship and will serve in a rural area. Dr. Pinchney says that we will have to make many of these decisions for ourselves. There won't be anybody around for referral."

Dr. Mann: "Dr. Pinchney does not know the practice of medicine. He hasn't had my experience."

There was silence in the room for a minute. The professor of biochemistry said something about the case and then dismissed the group. Several students stood by while Dr. Mann turned to Dr. Pinchney and said:

> **Dr. Mann:** "I'm glad we had a chance to correct the misinterpretation of that young man."
>
> **Dr. Pinchney:** "Well, he was correctly interpreting what I had said in class last week."
>
> **Dr. Mann:** "Well, then you are as wrong as he is. I've known medicine for thirty years, and this is the way it is done."
>
> **Dr. Pinchney:** "I believe that some men are making some changes now."
>
> **Dr. Mann:** "They are not changing what is right. I know what is right, and I am telling you what is right. You won't get me to back down on my convictions. I will do what is right for the patient every time."

Dr. Mann walked out of the room and left Dr. Pinchney standing with five medical students. The students began to express their support for Dr. Pinchney's position and to express sympathy for the "reaming" that he was receiving from the senior professor. Dr. Pinchney told the students to keep things quiet and went to his office.

Next morning, Dr. Pinchney called on Dr. Mann in his office.

> **Dr. Pinchney:** "We need to talk about these disagreements before students. The students feel

that you are putting me down. I think that a gulf is being created between us. I would like for us to develop more objectivity in talking about diagnosis and treatment procedures."

Dr. Mann: "I'm glad that you came by. I am distressed by your lack of objectivity. You are getting too personally involved in these clinical conferences."

Dr. Pinchney: "I guess that I am. But, when you continually say that your point is right and always refer to thirty years experience, I am frustrated to death."

Dr. Mann: "Why don't you listen to what I tell you? There will be plenty of time for you to learn—"

Dr. Pinchney [interrupting]: "I prefer to be independent in my conclusions, thank you."

Dr. Mann: "I don't think that you are. You blurt out what you think and then you are anxious to know what I will say. You are very dependent."

Dr. Pinchney: "I don't think so—"

Dr. Mann: "Oh, you make a show of independence in public, but you know that you cannot really back up your opinions by experience."

Dr. Pinchney: "I don't think that experience always makes a man right. You always argue that you are right. If your argument does not succeed then you fall back on experience and you keep talking in front of students about my inexperience."

Dr. Mann: "If you were more sensitive to my

needs, I would not need to remind you so much about this. I don't want to hurt you personally. You are a fine young man and a promising teacher, but you rush into these clinical conferences without consultation. We know beforehand the cases that we are going to present and we could talk about them on the day before the consultation. Then we would be together in our presentation to the students."

Dr. Pinchney: "Well, I guess we have a different point of view about teaching here. I like to work things out in front of the students so that they will see how people in our profession arrive at a decision. If we go in with a decision already made, they will think it is cut-and-dried."

Dr. Mann: "These students are young and easily confused. There is so much to teach them that we cannot tell them how we arrive at every decision. Some things are just *taught*."

Dr. Pinchney: "Well, I guess we just have a different idea about teaching."

Dr. Mann: "It's more than a difference of ideas. It's basically a question of confidence. I must tell you that I have serious doubts about your competence as a classroom leader. You wander off into so many things that are far away from our basic subject. Men are not going to know anatomy when they have finished a year with you."

Dr. Pinchney: "I don't like being called incompetent."

Dr. Mann: "Well, that is what you have become in this last year. I think you face a major ethical decision. Are you going to continue as a professor of anatomy when you really do not care about the subject that you are teaching?"

Dr. Pinchney: "I care about the relevance of anatomy to the practice of medicine. That's what I have tried to communicate in these weekly clinical seminars."

Dr. Mann: "Well, you have not done what you ought to have done. I know this subject and have taught it longer than you have been a doctor. As far as I am concerned, you have lost interest in a subject that is basic to medcine. I warn you, you are being unethical, and I will not stand for it. I have a committee meeting now, so I must go. I hope this all works out for us. I care very deeply about your future."

Dr. Mann walked out of the office and across the hall to a committee meeting. Dr. Pinchney decided to go home and tell his wife what had happened.

When he finished a recital of his difficulties, his wife was furious. For several hours, they alternated between anger and frustration. Now, what could he say or do to protect himself in this dangerous situation? The wife suggested that he talk to Dr. Roth again.

The next day Dr. Pinchney sat down in Dr. Roth's office and told of the previous day's conversation with Dr. Mann.

Dr. Roth: I know what you are up against.

It has happened before. Most men want to fight it out. You could try that, but you have a formidable opponent. Or you can leave. If so, the question is, what will you say when you leave?"

Dr. Pinchney: "Well, I would like to stay because I think that I represent a new point of view that is catching on with students. They listen to what I say, and they learn something."

Dr. Roth: "Sure, sure. Look, you wouldn't have any trouble with Charles [Mann] if you had not become popular. He can't stand that."

Dr. Pinchney: "So, what am I supposed to do?"

Dr. Roth: "Well, you could knuckle under and listen to what he has to say. That will be quite humiliating I know. You're probably too proud for that and probably have too much ability. But, if you want to stay here, that's the best way to stick it out."

Dr. Pinchney: "You're right. I'm too proud to do that. I wouldn't have this trouble if I had not given out my own opinions so often."

Dr. Roth: "Well, I have seen men badly hurt that way, and I guess you have those feelings also. What are you going to do with them?"

Dr. Pinchney: "I don't know. Right now I want to keep quiet and think this through."

A week later Dr. Mann walked down the hall with Dr. Pinchney after the clinical conference. He said, "I am proud

of you. You have not talked with anyone about our disagreements. I have checked around, and I find that neither
students nor faculty know that I had to say some hard
things to you. I hope we can work things out. I think
very highly of you."

Dr. Pinchney said, "Thank you," and went into his office. A few minutes later he was called to a departmental
meeting. Five professors sat down together under the chair-
manship of Dr. Mann. Dr. Mann explained that it was
time to do some new things in teaching. Rigid departmental lines should be unloosed and interdisciplinary studies
should be encouraged.

> **Dr. Mann:** "To begin this new process, I have
> recommended to the dean that we continue the
> weekly seminar on clinical practice for first-year
> students. Local practitioners should be brought
> in to this seminar to share their experience with
> the students. I know of Dr. Pinchney's interest
> in the relationship of first-year studies to the
> practice of medicine, so I have recommended
> him to the dean as the coordinator for this pro-
> gram. Since it will demand a good deal of time,
> he will be relieved of all duties as professor of
> anatomy. Now, are there any other matters that
> we need to take up as a department?"

There was silence, and then Dr. Mann dismissed the
meeting. Another assistant professor walked with Dr. Pinchney to his office and closed the door behind them.

Assistant Professor: "Are you going to let the old man get away with this? He has already told the students that you want to take this new seminar and have lost interest in anatomy. They don't know what is going on. They suspect that he is trying to move you out, but they don't know for sure. Are you just going to take this?"

Dr. Pinchney: "Yes, I am. My wife and I had a long talk about this the other night, and I have done lots of thinking since a conservation with Dr. Roth. There's nothing I could do but create a bad scene for the whole practice of medicine seminar. It's something that needs to be continued. I would like to stay and continue it, but I can't fight Mann by myself. I know the dean will support Mann and so will most of the senior faculty members. It would just be a grand mess if I protested his decision."

Assistant Professor: "I guess you're right. He has told several of us 'privately' that you have lost interest in anatomy and need to be in some related field. If you don't make that move, he will accuse you of incompetence to the dean."

Dr. Pinchney: "Yes, I know. He has already threatened me with that."

Assistant Professor: "So what are you going to do? Are we going to have to stay here and put up with this? At least six of us are sick and tired of what he has been doing. You are more popular with students than any of the rest of us. If you stay and fight, we might be able to do something."

Dr. Pinchney: What would happen to the interdisciplinary course during that fight?

Assistant Professor: "O.K., O.K. I just don't see how you can take it quietly."

Dr. Pinchney: "Well, I guess I just care very much about the profession of medicine. I dislike these personal quarrels among doctors. Students have a right to see something better in their professors. If men can't disagree about clinical matters in an objective fashion, then they should part company. I remember in med school that Dr. _____ did not speak to Dr. _____ for three years. Everybody knew it. I thought one of them should have left or they should reconcile their difficulties. There's no reconciliation here unless I knuckle under, and I'm too stubborn to do that. Anyway, we have a good course started, and Mann will continue it in some way."

Assistant Professor: "That's right. It really has caught on. The students have a scoring system in which each lecturer gets one point every time that he says something relevant to the practice of medicine. You really have changed things by getting that emphasis into gross anatomy. I must say I admire your willingness to put things like that ahead of your own feelings concerning that [characterization deleted]."

Dr. Pinchney: "Well, I'm idealistic, but I'm

also practical. If I keep my mouth shut and leave quietly there won't be any further attack from Dr. Mann. I couldn't keep quiet if I stayed, and if I continued to oppose him, he would ruin both me and the course I've developed. So, a quiet move seems to be the best solution."

The assistant professor shook his head and went out. Dr. Pinchney began to think of classmates to whom he could write about a new position.

Survival Through Surrender

Dr. Pinchney has made a decision that fits his ideals and personality. His goals are new teaching methods rather than his present security in this academic position. Of course, Dr. Pinchney formulates those ideals in terms of the group that is most significent to him. He hopes to do the best thing for medical students and the reputation of medical professors. But beyond that limited group is a larger purpose. He has developed a seminar that relates an academic subject to the actual practice of medicine. His question is, how does this teaching help people? This is an ideal that transcends both his personal security and the status of his profession.

Unfortunately, the young professor is aggressive and proud. This is one reason that he has come so quickly into combat with the establishment in his school. A different man might have accepted and acted upon the advice of Dr. Roth. But, Dr. Pinchney cannot be humble.

His saving grace is hope. He believes in something that

carries him through the temporary humiliation of silence before a jealous colleague. Therefore, he does not panic and loose sight of what is happening to himself and those around him. He has some insightful answers to the question: "What happens when I'm involved?"

Question	Answer
What's in this decision for me?	Demonstration of a new teaching method.
Should I show how I really feel?	He declares what he believes without appearing belligerant to Dr. Mann. He "tells all" to those who care and can take it: Dr. Roth and Ruth (wife).
Can I see myself in action?	Partially, but Dr. Roth, wife, and colleagues pinpoint difficulties—like humility.
Will I listen when I'm attacked?	To Dr. Roth yes, but Dr. Mann's warnings fall on deaf ears, since Dr. Pinchney doesn't respect his opinions anymore.

There is prudence in Dr. Pinchney's decision to surrender his position in order to survive personally. He knows that he cannot take responsibility for remaking the med school. Students and other assistant professors may urge this, but it does not seem realistic. Let's check on his performance:

Question	*Answer*
Am I honest with myself?	He admits that he's too proud to knuckle under for another year.
Am I frank with others?	He tells the students to be quiet because they could get hurt, but he states feelings and decisions openly to colleagues.
Why do I take this action?	The young doctor wants to continue his career without rumor that he's insubordinate.
Should I act now?	He's established a new viewpoint in teaching; if he stays the ideal will be lost in a personal conflict.

Living Beyond Yourself

An assistant professor told Dr. Pinchney: "Disagreeing with Dr. Mann is like looking down the barrel of a cannon—then BOOM!"

For this young executive, two aspects of bravery were required. One was the ability to go in and talk to a powerful colleague about their differences. The other was an optimistic spirit despite his defeat. He could tell students and colleagues that some new points of view were starting in the med school and that they would not be lost with his "retirement."

Question	Answer
Did he count the cost?	He decided that a transfer would be less costly than an interpersonal faculty conflict, and he couldn't be patient and humble.
Was he rewarded?	He sounds satisfied with a colleagues' statement that he is able to leave quietly, and elaborates on his higher objectives.
Did he listen for feedback?	He was consistently interested in the reports of Dr. Roth.
Was he cheerful?	Well, at least he was hopeful.

Dr. Pinchney's answers always pointed beyond his immediate situation to the values in medicine of what he was trying to do. In this he had the same spirit as experienced business executives who found that successful managers appeared to have deep resources on which to draw in time of difficulty or when some long-range decision must be made.

What the young professor lacks is one of the essential characteristics of a senior executive, temperance. He's moving in that direction in the self-control he shows with medical students, colleagues, and confrontations with Dr. Mann. But he did not restrain his self-assertiveness enough to ease by the prejudices of a powerful department chairman. Or we could say that his sense of integrity prevented him from keeping silent. Who knows? Anyway, he did start out with a rush. The fulfilment of his own objectives brought out the fears of a person on whom he had to depend for a few years. Since he was unwilling to wait, "knuckle under" while others gathered strength to support his view, he chose a prudent alternative. Movement to another situation would separate two stubborn and aggressive professors before they ruined an entire program.

Fortunately, the young doctor has learned one of the key questions of senior executives: "What do I want people to remember about me that will last?" That which is really worthwhile to him is not a tenured position or the defeat of an adversary, but the demonstration that his method of teaching can help other people. Somewhere inside of him is a belief that God approves that belief and that a man can walk securely from one position to another because the world has a place for his point of view.

That faith and hope is basic to the motivation and behavior of successful executives. We can't always put it into words, but when moral managers and their wives are asked why they act with prudence, temperance and fortitude, they usually come close to the spirit that was summarized by the prophet Micah: "What does the Lord require of you but to do justice, and to love kindness, and to walk humbly with your God"? (Micah 6:8, RSV).

Appendix

The Definition of Personal Morality

I. Meaning

Personal morality is a self-conscious attempt to regard the whole of life from the view of decision, self-determination, freedom, and responsibility. (Emil Brunner, *The Divine Imperative,* p. 26) Modern Roman Catholic "moral theologians" base personal morality upon Thomas Aquinas' definition of virtue as "a settled disposition of doing good." (Waldo Beach and H. Richard Niebuhr, *Christian Ethics,* p. 205) The most important American treatise on personal morality by Jonathan Edwards, defined virtue as "the duty of the qualities and exercises of the heart, or those actions which proceed from them." This was an eighteenth-century definition in Edward's paper on "The Nature of True Virtue" (*ibid.,* p. 390.)

"Virtue" is seldom used in modern studies of personal morality. Instead, a more common term is "value." In *The Value Issue of Business,* Alvaro Elbing defines value as a "concept of the desirable." He is influenced toward this definition by the anthropological studies of Clyde Kluckhohn, who contributed to sociologically oriented studies of organizations. Kluckhohn wrote: "A value is a conception, explicit or implicit, distinctive of an individual or characteristic of a group, of the desirable which influences the selection from available modes, means and ends of action." (In Talcott Parsons and Edward Shills, Editors, *Toward A General Theory of Action,* p. 395.)

In philosophy, "morals" and "morality" are still in general use and usually sum up the whole human situation in conduct and evaluation of conduct when "is" and "ought" must be brought together. (Crane Brinton, *A History of Western Morals,* p. 4-5.)

The origin of the concept of personal morality for western thought would be in the individualistic ethic of self-realization in Aristotle and in the ethical imperative of ideas in Plato. The Platonic Ideas "came from God" and have been the basis for modern assertions that morality originates in the will of God. So, for example Emil Brunner, a Swiss theologian maintained in the 1940s that morality is obedience to the perfect will of God. (Brunner, *op cit,* p. 88.) "Value" is looked upon by conservative theologians as a statement of conduct which is controlled by the inclination of men rather than by duty to God. It is this last meaning that is most current in management, thought, and literature. Chester Barnard, who was the first management writer to recognize that the leader must express the ideals of his group (according to Abraham Collier, *Harvard Business Review,* January-February 1953, p. 30) identified morals with "the ability to inhibit, control and modify immediate desires and impulses so that rational processes of deliberation may control the individual." (Chester Barnard, *Functions of the Executive,* p. 261.)

This definition by Barnard contains a mixture of duty and inclination. On the one hand, executives are expected to behave according to general principles of morality, which are usually identified in the *Harvard Business Review* and other management text with the "Judaeo-Christian tradition." On the other hand, it is asserted that a high sense of personal morality goes with success in management. Barnard, for example states that moral creativeness is the distinguishing mark of executive responsibility. It is the inventing of a moral basis for the solution of moral conflicts (*ibid.,* p. 276).

Barnard's definition is close to that adopted by the United States House of Bishops (Roman Catholic) in 1960. They stated that morality in business is "personal responsibility" *(Catholic Thought in Business Ethics,* p. 112).

The nouns "virtue," "morality," or "ethics" are seldom clear except in the context of a particular writer. We do not know if the origin of the term is considered to be in some divine command or in the natural order of things or in the goodness of a human being. The term is especially elusive in management writing, where personal morality may be equated with everything from enlightened self-interest to a workable application of Christian doctrine. Donald Shriver, who was Director of the Experimental Study of Religion and Society at North Carolina State University, was probably wise to refuse any specific definition of ethics or morality during the years of his discussions about "the ethic of responsibility" with businessmen in the southeast. ("Business Ethics and Religious Ethics," *Religion in Life,* Autumn, 1969.)

However, in most business articles we can distinguish personal morality as a reference to some self-conscious doctrine of conduct based on ultimate principles which characterize it as "right."

Some textbooks provide sophisticated definitions which also are useful for purposes of measuring the concept. *Management: Principles and Practices* defines "norms" as an obligation commonly acknowledged by a number of members of a group that the member ought to behave in certain ways under certain circumstances. Values describe what individuals consider important. Ethics are considerations of right and wrong conduct in the practical affairs of men (pp. 601-604). A clinical psychologist, Milton Rokeach has provided a more specific definition of value as "an enduring belief that a specific mode of conduct or end-state of existence is personally and socially preferable to alternative modes of conduct or end-states of existence." He has developed a list of "instrumental values" and "terminal values." The former refers to the way in which people move toward a desirable end, as with honesty or courage. The latter refers to some goal of existence, such as salvation or a world at peace (Milton Rokeach, "A Theory of Organization and Change Within Value-Attitude Systems," *The Journal of Social Issues,* January 1968, p. 16-17).

II. Utility

The concept of personal morality has moved from a side issue in the scientific management of Frederick W. Taylor to the central theme of Barnard in 1938 and to the title of Robert Golembiewski's, *Men, Management and Morality* in 1965. However, it should be noted that Golembiewski's writing is concerned with the development of organizational practices that are consistent with general ethical principles of the Judaeo-Christian tradition. He is not specifically concerned with inner sources of moral character in managers.

This latter concern, the inner sources of personal virtue, was more clearly and popularly stated by O. A. Ohmann in a *Harvard Business Review* article that first appeared in the 1950s and was reprinted in January-February, 1970, as a Harvard Classic. It appears from the reception of this article that personal responsibility, conceived of as moral obligation and personal virtue is becoming a primary concept in some management circles.

Some new uses of old terms may be seen in the current interest of public administrators in the writings of John Rawls, *A Theory of Justice.* Rawls seemed to equate the "good" with terminal values and the "right" with instrumental values. In most business literature, values or virtues are often looked upon as something from the past that must be called up and redefined in the present. (See for example O. A. Ohmann's "Search for Managerial Philosophy" *Harvard Business Review,* September-October, 1957 p. 46.)

Personal values (or morality) have often been considered in relation to the concept of executive traits. There is some blending of "traits" and character in Perrin Stryker *The Character of the Executive: Eleven Studies in Managerial Qualities.*

The idea of personal morality must also be integrated into the general concept of social responsibility. Reinhold Niebuhr has warned that self-interest grows in group relations until it becomes a collective egoism. The individual inclination toward the good is diffused and often perverted in the complex world of society *(Moral Man and Immoral Society,* p. XI, XX and 36-37). He concludes that civilization has become a device for delegating the vices of individuals to larger and larger communities *(ibid.,* p. 49).

The categories of personal morality are either considered in the medieval typology of the cardinal virtues (prudence, temperance, bravery, and justice) or in more modern thought as a series of questions. The basic question is "what ought I to do?" This is the question of duty, the beginning of personal responsibility. The second question is "for what am I responsible?" This is the question of purpose or commitment. What is considered to be the best in our lives? Then there is a third question "what am I responsible *for?*" This implies some decision between various moral objectives that might be chosen at a particular time. Is a person to think first of parents, God, country, neighbors? What is the most "fitting" action? These are the questions that are considered extensively by James Gustafson in *Christ and the Moral Life* and in chapters by H. Richard Niebuhr and others in a symposium *On Being Responsible* edited by Gustafson and James T. Laney.

On the question of minimizing or maximizing personal values, Edmund Learned and associates concluded that there are spiritual implications in all business actions. Therefore, it would not be possible to minimize something which is so integral to the decision-making process of modern industry. In fact, he found that every major speaker at the Fiftieth Anniversary Conference of the Harvard Business School Association in 1958 stressed the importance of more attention to spiritual values ("Personal Values in Business Decisions" *Harvard Business Review,* March-April 1959, p. 112).

However, there are a number of serious questions to be considered in an executive's understanding of personal morality. Perhaps the most basic difficulty is between morality as enlightened self-interest and morality as a search for the good of *all* beings in their inter-relationships. The former is stressed by Albert Carr in "Can an Executive Afford a Conscience?" *(Harvard Business Review,* July-August 1970, p. 58-60). The latter is a basic tenet of Jonathan Edwards (Beach, *op cit,* p. 387). Reinhold Niebuhr seeks to resolve the problem by noting that spiritual values must rest upon a realistic assessment of man as an incomplete person. He cannot serve the interest of all people in the best way. Instead, he must balance self-interest with concern for the community. Moral perfection is not possible in the real world.

Another distinguished theologian, Samuel Miller wrote in the January 1960 issue of the *Harvard Business Review* that an oversimplified solution to business ethics would stress unselfishness. This insinuates an emotional factor into a situation that may smooth over the real difficulty by some misguided act of self-denial. The basic problem to be explored has then been covered by unreality. Mr. Miller, Dean of the Harvard Divinity School saw the difficulty in a common assumption that men are expected to be perfect if they are Christian. He considers this to be an impossibility.

The central issue in the use of "personal morality" in management is an awareness of the limited ability of individuals to accomplish that which is "good." Categories of personal morality may be used to *approximate* the good in a particular situation. This is commonly described today as "situation ethics," of whom the most provocative champion is Joseph Fletcher *(Situation Ethics)*. In business circles, the situation ethics report has been blended into the case study, as in the "Crisis in Conscience at Quasar" article in the *Harvard Business Review* for March-April, 1968, and the "Sequel to Quasar Stellar" in the September-October, 1968, issue of the same magazine.

Bibliography on Personal Morality in Business

Alford, Raphael D., "Business and the Good Society," *Harvard Business Review,* July-August 1965. Given the nature of business how can we cut the cost of freedom and control the excesses of vitality? Conscience inevitably slows down action; responsibility checks flexibility.

Barnard, Chester, *Functions of the Executive,* Cambridge: Harvard University Press, 1960. Executive responsibility is the capacity of leaders to invent a moral basis for the solution of conflicts that go beyond technical decisions in such a way that other members of the organization feel compelled to give their assent and support to these objectives.

Baumhart, Raymond C., "How Ethical are Businessmen?" *Harvard Business Review,* July-August 1961. Seventeen hundred Harvard Business Review Executive readers answered questions about ethics in business.

Bennett, John C. et. al., *Christian Values and Economic Life,* New York: Harper and Bros., 1954. Protestant businessmen and theologians discuss Christian ethics and the forms of economic power, economic life and economic problems.

Childs, Marquis and Douglass Cater, *Ethics in a Business Society.* New York: Harper and Bros., 1954. As part of a series of conferences of the Dept. of Church and Economic Life of the Federal Council of Churches, the history of economic theory and development is reviewed from a philosophical point of view.

Gustafson, James M., *Christ and the Moral Life,* New York: Harper and Row, 1968. "What Ought I To Do?" The author discusses the nature and source of "good," the character of the person who has the right to do good and the criteria for judging proper actions. The theological goal is conformity to the life of Christ.

Gustafson, James M. and James T. Laney, Editors, *On Being Responsible: Issues In Personal Ethics,* New York: Harper Forum Books, 1968. The theory and practice of personal morality is discussed by Roman Catholic and Protestant theologians.

Hobson, J. A., *Economics and Ethics: A Study of Social Values.* New York: B. C. Heath, 1929. The process of production and consumption are traced in relation to human welfare and the rising demand for ethical considerations in economics and the control of economic processes by organized society.

Hyneman, Knight F., *The Ethics of Competition and Other Essays.* New York: Augustus Kelley, 1935. Competition as a game in business is contrasted with the pagan ethics of duty or perfection and the Christian ideal of spirituality. Additional essays consider economic theory and nationalism, interest in value, the scientific method in economics, and marginal utility.

Leys, Wayne, *Ethics for Policy Decisions.* New York: Prentice-Hall, 1952. After reviewing the major questions asked by philosophical moralists, the author considers a variety of applications of morals, including those to policy decisions in business.

Niebuhr, Reinhold, *Moral Man and Immoral Society*. New York: Charles Scribner's Sons, 1932. The ability of an individual to be moral in society is diminished by the complexity of decisions that must be made in modern culture.

Ohmann, O. A., "Sky Hooks" *Harvard Business Review,* January-February, 1970. A manager with sound values is necessary to set the climate within which values become working realities in an organization. This intergrative function is the core of the administrator's contribution.

Rokeach, Milton, "A Theory of Organization and Change Within Value-Attitude systems, " *The Journal of Social Issues,* January 1968. Values have to do with enduring guides for action by an individual. They may be classified as instrumental (means) and terminal (ends) and items can be constructed for a test to measure both of these.

Selekman, Sylvia Kopald and Benjamin M., *Power and Morality in a Business Society*. New York: McGraw-Hill, 1956. The moral involvement of power calls for a new look at management. It means doing things with people as equals and not for them as inferiors.

Selekman, Benjamin, *A Moral Philosophy for Management*. New York: McGraw-Hill, 1959. The new problem of business is how to relate the ought of ethics to the must of technical production. The goal is a decentralized industrial system manned by individuals of high purpose responsive to the ethics of the Judaeo-Christian tradition.

Stryker, Perrin, *The Character of the Executive*. New York: Harper, 1960. Eleven qualities of a manager are dramatized.